M. Mayer

Hours of Devotion

A Book of Prayers and Meditations for the Use of the Daughters of Israel.

Fifth Edition

M. Mayer

Hours of Devotion

A Book of Prayers and Meditations for the Use of the Daughters of Israel. Fifth Edition

ISBN/EAN: 9783337255282

Printed in Europe, USA, Canada, Australia, Japan

Cover: Foto ©Lupo / pixelio.de

More available books at **www.hansebooks.com**

HOURS OF DEVOTION.

A BOOK OF

PRAYERS AND MEDITATIONS

FOR THE USE OF

THE DAUGHTERS OF ISRAEL,

DURING PUBLIC SERVICE AND AT HOME. FOR ALL CONDITIONS OF WOMAN'S LIFE.

Translated from the German *"Stunden der Andacht"*

BY

M. MAYER.

FIFTH EDITION.

HEBREW PUBLISHING CO.

NEW YORK.

INDEX.

	PAGE.
Prayers on entering the Synagogue	7
Morning Prayer	8
Night Prayer	9
Prayer before retiring to bed	11
Morning Prayer for children	12
Evening Prayer for children	13

DAILY PRAYERS.

		PAGE
Prayer for Sunday		14
"	for Monday	15
"	for Tuesday	16
"	for Wednesday	16
"	for Thursday	17
"	for Friday	18
"	on the Eve of the Sabbath	20
"	for the Sabbath Day	22
"	when the law is taken out	23
Meditation on the holy Sabbath		24
Prayer for the close of the Sabbath		25
"	on the Sabbath previous to the New Moon	26
"	for the Day of New Moon	27

FESTIVAL PRAYERS.

Prayer for the First Days of Passover		28
"	for the Last Days of Passover	30

	PAGE
Prayer for the Feast of Weeks.—(Pentecost)	31
Meditation on the Decalogue	33
Prayer for the Anniversary of the Destruction of the Temple (תשעה באב)	38
Prayer for the month of Ellul	43
" for the Eve of New Year	44
" for the New Year's Day	47
Meditation for the New Year's Day and the Day of Atonement	49
Prayer on the Eve of the Day of Atonement (כל נדרי)	52
" for the Day of Atonement	54
" for the Evening of Atonement (נעילה)	61
" for the Departed (הזכרת נשמות)	64
" for the First Day of Tabernacles	65
Prayer for the 8th Day of Tabernacles (שמיני עצרת)	67
" for the Day of Rejoicing of the Law (שמחת תורה)	70
Prayer for the Feast of Chanuccah	71
" for the Feast of Purim	73

PRAYERS FOR MAIDENS.

Prayer for a young Maiden	74
" for an Orphan	76
" for a Bride on her Nuptial Day	76

PRAYERS FOR MARRIED WOMEN.

A Wife's Prayer for Matrimonial Happiness	77

	PAGE

A Mother's Prayer on the Wedding Day of her Daughter 78
A Mother's Prayer on the Wedding Day of her Son 79
Prayer on the approach of Accouchement. 80
" after save delivery 81
" for a Mother on visiting the Synagogue after Confinement 82
Prayer for a Childless Wife. 83
A Mother's Prayer at the Confirmation of her Children............................... 84
A Mother's Prayer whose child is abroad...... 86
A Wife's Prayer whose Husband is on a Journey 87
A Widow's Prayer.. 87

MISCELLANEOUS PRAYERS.

A Child's Prayer for his Parents.............. 88
Prayer for Patience and Strength in Adversity.. 90
Thanksgiving for Deliverance 91
Prayer during a Voyage...................... 92
During a Storm at Sea....................... 93
Prayer at the End of a Voyage................ 94

PRAYERS FOR THE SICK.

Prayer for a Sick Husband................... 95
" for Sick Parents...................... 95
" for a Sick Child 96
" in Heavy Sickness................... 97

PRAYERS FOR THE DEAD.

Prayer on the Anniversary of a Parents Death
    (Jahrzeit)............................. 98
   "   at a Father's Grave................... 99
   "   at a Mother's Grave 100
   "   at a Husband's Grave.................102
   "   at the Grave of a Child............. 104
   "   at the Grave of a Brother or Sister. .105

HOURS OF DEVOTION.

PRAYER ON ENTERING THE SYNAGOGUE.

I greet thee, thou holy, silent habitation, thou goodly Temple of the Lord! Be blessed, ye consecrated halls! Here dwells and reigns the Lord,—here mine eye beholds the glory of the Almighty,—His majesty hovers around me,—I am encompassed by His holiness.

Bent down and worn out by the cares of life I pass the threshold of this Sanctuary, and behold! the spirit of peace takes possession of my heart! Sorrow vanishes, and the anxiety of my soul yields to fervent and tearful prayer. *"Truly, this is the house of God, and here is the gate that leads into heaven!"*

Merciful God! Thou art nigh unto me everywhere, but nearest unto me in this place. Here, I feel safe and secure beneath Thy protecting hand, O Heavenly Father! Here, I feel myself shielded against the temptations and vicissitudes of life;—here, my soul willingly offers up its sacrifices, my life is cheerfully placed at Thy disposal, who art my Creator and Savior;—here, I disclose unto Thee my most secret desires, my inmost inclinations. Out there, in the bustle and turmoil of the world, life, with its temptations and allurements, with its burthens and obstacles, rises like a barrier between my heart and Thee, my Lord! but upon my entrance into these silent, still, and sacred halls, that barrier vanishes, and my soul rises unto Thee; full of fervor and enthusiasm, full of inspiring awe and devotion, I feel myself purer and better, for virtue and religion appear unto me in their sublime and heavenly form, in their eternal, unchangeable majesty. My heart widens, my innermost soul becomes radiant with light, my very thoughts and emotions become sanctified,—sinful passions vanish and make room for good, noble and virtuous resolves.

Oh! may these lofty sentiments, this lucid contemplation of Thee, my Lord and Creator, never be dimmed, and may the consecration and holiness, which here permeate my heart, follow me into life without; and may this hour become unto me an hour of bliss and grace, an hour of acceptance, and pleasing in Thine eyes, O merciful and benign Father! Amen.

MORNING PRAYER.

All-gracious, All-merciful God! Thy paternal goodness has permitted me to awaken after a refreshing sleep, and has sent the gladdening rays of morning to revive me anew.

O Heavenly Father! how great is the mercy which Thou hast shown unto me. My first emotion is, therefore, to thank Thee, from the innermost depth of my heart, for Thy providential watchfulness over my life, and for having protected me whilst the darkness of night surrounded me.

How many of my fellow-creatures but yesternight ascended the couch in good health and hopes, and yet cannot leave it this day, from being bound to it by pains and suffering! how many may have yesternight sunk to sleep amidst riches and affluence, but who are brought to poverty this morning by sudden disaster. Alas! how many others are languishing, perhaps, in the dark gloom of a prison, into which no friendly ray of joy penetrates. And how large may be the number of those who fell asleep last night, never to awaken any more in this world.

How thankful ought I therefore to be, Heavenly Creator! for Thy goodness, wherewith Thou hast warded off every danger from me, hast preserved my health, and restored me to the arms of my relations and friends. Oh! let me ever cherish this feeling of gratitude within my heart, so that I may faithfully discharge my religious and domestic duties; that I may meet my fellow-creatures with loving-kindness, such as Thou hast shown unto me; and that I may ever extol Thee, who causest the sleeper to awake, and who wilt cause those that sleep the sleep of death to awake to eternal life. Amen.

NIGHT PRAYER.

Father of All! again a day has passed, and night spread her sombre mantle over the earth. Nature rests, and man, following her example, sinks into the embrace of refreshing sleep. But before closing mine eyes in slumber, I raise them in gratitude unto Thee, my Creator; ere I shall deliver my thoughts and feelings unto the power of sleep, let my heart and life engage in communion with Thee.

My soul delights to think of Thee, O Eternal Father! who, like a father, carest for us in the fullness of love and mercy. *"How sweet is it to give thanks unto Thee, and to give praise unto Thy name, O Most High!"* Many are the benefits which I received this day,—many the gifts and blessings which Thou didst bestow upon me. Thou didst cause the light of heaven to shine upon me, and the splendor of the earth to enrapture mine eye; Thy loving kindness has gladdened me, Thy heavenly beneficence covered me with the wings of love, and Thy merciful hand sustained me and carried me through many evils and dangers that surrounded me. All joy and cheerfulness came from Thee, and in the dark hour of grief, thou didst take my wearied head to Thy parental heart and uphold me with heavenly comfort.

Therefore, my soul is full of gratitude, my lips utter Thy praise, my heart trusts in Thee lovingly and confidingly, O Thou Unsearchable One! who always *givest* and never *receivest*, who continually dispensest blessings, and who art the inexhaustible Fountain of goodness and mercy. Truly, Thou art a God of infinite love and grace. But with fear and trembling I ask the questions: Have I, by my works and action during the past day, made myself acceptable unto Thy grace? Have I faithfully and properly fulfilled my duties towards Thee and my fellow-men? Have I not neglected to perform deeds of charity, of love and of mercy? And whenever I have performed them, have I done so with a perfect heart and in a proper spirit, or in a cold, unfriendly manner? Have I served Thee, my God! with all my heart—have I trusted in Thee,—have I reverenced and feared Thee? Have I withstood all temptations, folly and sin?

With grief and repentance I must confess, I have sinned before Thee! I have not always borne Thee within my heart, I have not always walked in the path which Thou hast laid out for us. My thoughts have not always been sanctified, nor my passions subdued and controlled by Thy law. Oh, how I feel prostrated by the stings of my conscience! I recognize the utter hatefulness of sin, its demoralizing and degrading influence: depriving man of his choicest treasure, the peace and happiness of his soul. Oh! be merciful unto me, Thou God of mercy, who art abundant in love and compassion. Forgive my transgressions, O Lord! and turn not from me in anger, in this hour. Relieve the anxiety of my soul, and make peace and tranquillity, once more, to descend into my heart, that I may enjoy the blessing of sleep and repose, reconciled within my heart, reconciled with Thee, my God, and with my conscience.

Cause Thy love, O All-merciful God! to watch over me and guard me against the terrors and dangers that creep in darkness. Grant, O God! that the sleep which Thou hast sent down upon earth may be comfort to the oppressed, bring relief unto them that are prostrated by sufferings and sorrows, and pour its refreshing balm upon me and those endeared to my heart. Hide us under the shadow of Thy wings, thus we shall be secure ; for Thou, O God! art my banner, and a sure refuge unto me, my Fortress, my Rock, my Shield. Into Thy hand I commit my spirit and my body,—my peace and my happiness, all that is near and dear unto me in this life: *whether I am asleep or awake, God is with me, and I fear not*—Amen.

PRAYER BEFORE RETIRING TO BED.

Sleep—peaceful tender angel whom God hath sent down to this valley of tears, to cover with thy soft wings the suffering of life,—alight upon mine eyelids and rock me into repose ; enter the huts of misery, and cause sweet dreams to sport around the couch of the unhappy, that they may forget their sorrows and become unconscious of their woes. Bring healing unto the sick, that they may awake refreshed and strengthened and feel new, youthful vigor flow through their weary limbs,—and show unto all those who weep over a dear departed being, that death also is but a peaceful sleep, to be followed by a glorious waking up, a blissful rising in the realms of light, where there is no more night, nor the terror of darkness : but heavenly unutterable beatitude in the presence of God.

Beautiful and significant is the parable, that the soul leaves the weary body, its earthly abode, during the night, to inscribe into the great book of heaven the deeds done during the day;—and that, when on some future day, God shall summon man before His judgment seat, his own handwriting shall testify for or against him. O my soul! mayest thou have to record only noble thoughts and beneficent deeds upon that book of everlasting memorial—Amen.

MORNING PRAYER FOR CHILDREN.

O God! Thy goodness now I praise
   That did Thy child securely keep;
My grateful heart and eyes I raise
   To Thee who call'st me up from sleep.

O God! be Thou my helping friend,
   And guide me in the way of night;
From ev'ry sin my life defend
   Send to my soul Thy heav'nly light.

My parents, brothers, sisters dear
   Protect and shield beneath Thy love;
Awake or 'sleep, Thou, God, art near,
   To grant Thy blessings from above.

And pure as I commence this day,
   May I conclude it joyfully,—
With deeds that never pass away,
   But last unto eternity.

EVENING PRAYER FOR CHILDREN.

Now to bed I do retire,
   Rest to find and sweet repose;
Lord! my weary eyes aspire
   Unto Thee before they close.

Thou, O Father, ever good,
   Take my thanks for all Thy love,
For Thy care, for drink and food,
   Which Thou gav'st me from above.

Pardon ev'ry sinful deed,
   Ev'ry evil I have done;
Let my tender age now plead
   To Thy mercy, Holy One!

Let my childhood's innocence
   Last through life, unbroken, pure;
That, when'er thou call'st me hence,
   My salvation shall be sure.

DAILY PRAYERS.

FOR SUNDAY.

Hallelujah!—Praise ye God, the Eternal, who in His Omnipotence brought forth the world from nothing, and who by His merciful command "Let there be light," set a boundary to the darkness of chaos. Thanks to Thee, O Father, for the beneficial and all-rejoicing Light; thanks to Thee for this boon, so worthy of Thy greatness—a boon, the salutary influence of which I now also enjoy—that I may look up to Thee, O Father, with filial confidence, and that I may worship Thee with deep reverence

And since light was the first production which Thou, in Thine all-merciful greatness, calledst forth in Thy Creation, since light was the first, which, as we are taught by Holy Scripture, Thou hast deigned to designate a *good* gift: may it be Thy will, O all-gracious Father, that this great boon may rejoice and cheer me also, Thy handmaiden, whilst I live; and that it may also serve me for that purpose, which was intended by Thy wisdom, for the whole community of mankind.

Grant also, O Lord! I beseech Thee, that the Light of Thy truth may guide, enlighten, and prosper me, that my spirit may not grope in the dark, and that I may not fall a prey to corruption. Grant, O All-merciful One! that the light of Thy sacred law may lead me in the path of virtue, that I may never deviate therefrom, but continue to ennoble my heart, and render myself ever worthier of Thy mercy, which, I trust, Thou wilt never withhold from me. Amen.

FOR MONDAY.

Hallelujah! Praise ye the Eternal, ascribe honor unto Him for evermore; exalt Him, ye nations, and sing of His glory, and His marvelous deeds. Like unto a tent He spread out the firmament over endless waters, and called it "Heaven." That Heaven declareth the Omnipotence of its Creator, though "not by speech nor by language." From yonder impenetrable heights He looketh down into the heart of every man, whose innermost thoughts He knoweth; ordaineth the steps of every human being; and rewardeth and punisheth the high as well as the low, the superior as well as the inferior, the rich as well as the poor. From yonder heights He compassionates the oppressed here beneath, and lifteth up those that are humbled down O Lord! may this thought continually be present unto my mind, that I may never, even when I stand on the summit of prosperity,—allow myself to be beguiled by vanity, pride, or eagerness for dazzling show; that I may never deny assistance to any one in need thereof, but follow Thee, O bengin Father, who art ever near to him, and helpeth him who calleth upon Thee in truth. For art Thou not the God that loveth humility but hateth pride? Art Thou not the Lord who said "the heaven is my throne, and the earth is my footstool,—but to this man will I look, even to him that is poor, and of a contrite spirit, and trembleth at my word?" Strengthen me also then, O merciful Father, in my resolve to support the fallen, and relieve the oppressed at all times, to the utmost, according to my means and powers, in order that I may render myself worthy of being numbered among the בני רחמנים "the childern of the compassionate," a name which ever distinguished Israel. Amen.

FOR TUESDAY.

Hallelujah! Praise thou, O my soul, the exalted Creator, who adorned the earth, which He gave to *all* men, with fruit-trees and herbs of every kind, on the third day of the creation. A mild congenial verdure decked the surface of the earth, which had but just emerged from the waters; valleys wrapped themselves in herbs and plants of thousand-fold colors, and of lovely fragrance; and thus was created the first Spring, which now returns in due season to the joy and delight of all living creatures, according to the laws which Thou, benign Father, hast prescribed for nature. Millions of powers developed themselves on that day of Creation, as soon as Thy mighty call, "Let there be," resounded. Millions of powers now proclaim Thine Omnipotence, so that every feeling heart joyfully and deeply moved, calleth unto Thee, "this is my God, and I will exalt Him." In the book of nature every one can reverentially read Thy paternal love; on the heights as well as in the depths, in the storm as well as in the calm, moves and waves the spirit of Thy love. Let, therefore, everything which hath breath in its nostrils, praise the Lord. Hallelujah.

FOR WEDNESDAY.

Hallelujah! Praise God in due meekness, praise Him, —declare His high exalted fame and glory. Myriads of heavenly bodies, suns, moons, and stars were created by His Omnipotence on the fourth day of creation, that in their lofty magnificence reverentially obey His law, and never trespass over the limits assigned to them. Al of these bodies,—the sun with his ocean of rays, the moon and the stars with their bright lustres, proclaim Thy glory, and call, "who among the mighty is like unto Thee, O Lord, who so glorified in holiness!" By those luminaries of heaven Thou, O all-wise Creator, didst divide the seasons of the year, didst fix the boundaries of day and night; therefore, shall my soul be uplifted to Thee in thankfulness, and sing praises unto Thy great name. When the beams of the sun break forth through the grey dawn, and spread light, warmth, life, and joy unto all, who then can resist thanking Thee from the innermost depths of the heart? When the moon with her lovely brightness softly lights up the dark night, accompanied by a choir of stars, what feeling heart of mortal is not then penetrated with emotions of gratefulness? who does not exclaim with amazement, "what is man that Thou, the Creator of so many worlds, rememberest him?" But Thou art also kind and merciful, O Father, towards all Thy creatures; wherefore, I also will ever comfort myself with the words of the inspired psalmist, "my help cometh from the Lord, who created the heavens and the earth." Amen.

FOR THURSDAY.

Hallelujah! Unto Thee exalted Creator of nature, shall resound my song of joy; unto Thee be ever dedicated my praise. Oh, soar up from thy mortal coil, my spirit, to the Creator of beings without number, to the Omnipotent, who on the fifth day of the Creation filled the earth, the waters, and the air with living creatures, all of which praise and exalt their Creator who at all times remembereth them, and who is a Father unto all of them. The inhabitants of thes paces of all spheres, as well as the great monsters of the sea, the high-soaring eagle, as well as the worm in the dust pay homage unto Thy Majesty. From the dawn of morning, until the coming forth of the evening-star on the heavens, these creatures all proclaim Thy grace and paternal care. And I, after having arrived at this conviction, should

I allow my trust in Thee to be weakened by timid doubts or chilled scoffing? No, O beloved Father! may neither the one nor the other ever deprive me of the hopes, that Thou wilt never forsake me, that Thou wilt never deliver me up to destruction. Even if the path of my life remain clouded in obscurity, doth not the voice, sounding like the melody of angels, call unto me, "I am the Eternal, thy God, I am with thee! I am thy refuge!" Yes, O Father, it is Thou who hast continually watched over me; it is Thou who hast vouchsafed Thy blessing unto all those who follow the path of the righteous, and whose efforts are directed to that purpose, more and more to resemble Thee in the pursuit of all that is good and virtuous, that I may exclaim with joy, יי לי לא אירא "the Eternal is with me, I fear nothing!" Amen.

FOR FRIDAY.

Thou art great, O God! in Thy visible wonders and works, but still greater in Thine invisible ordinations and dispensations.

In the six days of creation Thine almighty word called this great and beautiful earth into existence, the earth and whatever filleth it,—the animals and plants,—the refreshing dew and the lustrous stars. And when the world was finished in its glory, thou didst place man into it, that he may know all Thy glorious works, enjoy all created things, and praise Thee who art so good and gracious.

All-merciful Father! worlds praise Thee, choirs of angels sing everlasting hymns unto Thee,—and why should not man, the son of earth worship and praise Thee, since Thou hast thus distinguished him,—hast especially remembered and blessed him in Thy paternal love, hast honored and exalted him?

Yea, my God! I will adore Thee, and praise Thee by a life full of virtue, full of holiness and purity, full of reverence for God, and love for man; nor will I ever give myself up to sin or ingratitude towards Thy loving-kindness.

Thou hast formed and created man in Thine own image; Thou hast given him a body, beautiful and noble in shape and form—Thou hast given him a spirit still nobler and more exalted, a ray from Thy wisdom, a light of Thy love, and hast united both into one glorious, wonderful whole! And should I deface, destroy this masterpiece of creation, by sin and vice? should I disfigure my body by excesses and immorality, deprive it of its beauty by low desires, by unbridled passions, by malice, hatred, envy and jealousy? should I deprive my spirit of its nobility by vulgar sentiments and aspirations, by unholy, brutal practices? No, no! I will carefully watch over myself, ennoble my heart by acts of charity, elevate my spirit by Thy precepts and Thy divine Law; I will guard my body, this frail garb of the soul, against every pernicious influence, against every thing that may endanger its health, or weaken its energies; for it is the creation of Thy hands, the means and instrument of our labors upon earth!

Mayest Thou, O Lord, our God! aid me, and strengthen me in my resolves,—mayest Thou, O All-merciful One! guard me against all temptations, that want and suffering, grief and sorrow may never overpower me—that bodily affliction and pains may not bring untimely dimness upon the light of my soul, that mental grief and pangs may not too soon weaken and destroy my body;—that I may ever aspire heavenward, and sacrifice unto Thee the vigor of my spirit and the glow of my heart, until Thine inscrutable judgment shall separate my soul from my body, and my spirit wing its flight up to Thee, thenceforward to dwell

ON THE EVE OF THE SABBATH.

בָּרוּךְ אַתָּה יְיָ אֱלֹהֵינוּ מֶלֶךְ הָעוֹלָם אֲשֶׁר קִדְּשָׁנוּ בְּמִצְוֹתָיו וְצִוָּנוּ לְהַדְלִיק נֵר שֶׁל שַׁבָּת.

(*On Festivals:* נֵר שֶׁל יוֹם טוֹב and בִּרְכַּת שֶׁהֶחֱיָנוּ.)

Praised be Thou, O Eternal our God, King of the world, who hast sanctified us by Thy commandments and commanded us to light the lamp of Sabbath. (*On the eve of a Festival say:* The lights of the Feast.)

Almighty God! with joyful emotions I light, according to Thy command and behest, this lamp, as an ornament and glorification of the Sabbath hours which Thou hast consecrated and hallowed. How sweet, how precious are these hours which Thy grace has given us! Oh! how the calm stillness of Sabbath rejoice our hearts, affording recreation to the body for the toils and labors of the week-days, while the spirit soars up unto Thee on the wings of holy meditations, and the heart seeks and finds Thee in fervent prayer, in pious attention to the proclamation of Thy holy word, in undisturbed contemplation of Thy loving-kindness. Many are the cares and sorrows of the week-days, many the struggles in life, but when Sabbath appears, rest and peace enter our hearts;—the restless desires, the exciting aspiration and struggle after earthly gifts and treasures give way to sweet repose of the mind, and the heart is opened unto calm, pleasant and quieting emotions.

All-good Father! how can we sufficiently thank Thee for all Thy grace and goodness? Throughout the week Thou didst surround us with Thy protection and mercy; Thy paternal grace did bless us with life and health, with nourishment and garments to put on, with light and warmth; Thou didst prepare for us thousand pleasures which rejoiced our hearts, often even, ere we were aware thereof! From day to day, the Manna of Thy heavenly blessing came down for us;—and, at the end of the week, which has been so full of Thy manifold gifts, Thou grantest the choicest of all heavenly boons—the *Sabbath day*. *The Sabbath is the crown and glorious ornament of the week!* it ennobles our aspirations, consecrates our enjoyments, pours soft, heavenly light upon our pilgrim path on earth, and carries us *back* to Thee, whenever the aspirations of the week-days have *removed* us from Thee. We look up to Thee, O God! with pure confidence, in love and humility;—and every thought of Thee removes the veil from before our eyes,— the light increases within our souls, and we feel the certainty of a better future, of a higher Sabbath in Thy presence, where the weary pilgrim, in the lustrous light, beaming from Thy throne, enters upon everlasting rest,—where the gates of Eden are opened for the pious and righteous, who have accomplished their career, who have fulfilled the destination of their lives. And the heavier our labors shall have been on earth, the sweeter will be the fruit thereof,—the more industrious the laborer shall have been, the richer will be his reward.

Bless, then, O my God! these holy hours, that they may realize unto me also their elevating and quickening power,—that they may afford recreation and strength unto my body,—understanding and enlightenment unto my spirit, that I may more and more improve in the knowledge of Thee, and thus be enabled to walk in Thy ways, and become more and more worthy of Thy benevolence. Grant Thine almighty protection unto me and mine, guard us against all accident and evil,—aid Thou us to conquer every temptation and allurement of sin, and cause the light of joy to burn in our hearts, and the light of love and peace to shine in our homes.—Amen.

FOR THE SABBATH DAY.

Almighty God! with profound humility I would offer unto Thee the oblations of my gratitude for the precious gift of this holy day of bodily rest and spiritual elevation. After six days of toil and labor, this messenger of peace again and again appears unto us, to give strength unto the weary, freedom unto the enthralled, courage unto the oppressed, and teaches us, that Thine almighty protection accompanies us in the pilgrim paths of this earthly life, from its beginning even unto its end ; that Thou blessest the fruits of our labor, and bestowest upon us all that of which we stand in need ; that *"not by bread alone man doth live, but by every thing that proceedeth out of Thy mouth,"* by obedience to Thy holy Law, for the preservation and diffusion of which Thou didst deliver Israel from the Egyptian bondage, and hast guided them safely through all perils and sufferings even to this day.

Heavenly Father! we feel Thy blissful and quickening presence ; we hear the mighty voice of Thy spirit as in the endless Universe, so also in the course of our own destinies, and even in the longing of our soul that *"panteth after Thee, O Lord! as a hart panteth after brooks of water,"*—in the desire of our hearts to approach Thee, and take refuge from the billowing ocean of earthly life beneath the shadow of Thy protecting presence,—and all that is within us exults in Thee, Thou, Eternal God and Father! Thy mercy shall never forsake us, not even in death ! Through the darkness of the grave, Thou leadest the righteous unto the everlasting Sabbath, unto never-ending salvation !

"With honor and glory Thou hast crowned the son of man," and hast vested him, the most miraculous being of Thy creation, with freedom to choose between life and death. Oh ! mayest Thou also teach me to number my days, and

apply my heart unto wisdom Grant me a pure heart, a spirit permeated by Thy holy word, a life filled with deeds of love for Thee and my fellow-beings.

Help me, O God! to attend, on this holy Sabbath, with earnestness to the things that concern our everlasting peace; grant, that all my thoughts and actions may be holy and unblameable in Thy sight; fill me with the spirit of true devotion in the hours of worship and open my mind for the truths that may be proclaimed in Thy Holy Sanctuary. By attending upon the ordinances of our holy religion, on this day, may I grow wiser and better, purer and holier, more meek and humble, more resigned and thankful, and more heartily disposed to follow Thy sacred behests.

Speedily—we feel this—speedily as the days of the week, do our years vanish hence, and the work and work-days of this shadow-like existence will be ended, ere we be aware thereof;—Oh! may my soul, when my day of departure shall come, look back with contentment upon the removing shadows, hopefully soar to its Heavenly Source, and everlastingly walk in Thy light, my Rock and Redeemer! Amen

PRAYER, WHEN THE LAW IS TAKEN OUT.

Praised be the name of Him who, in His holiness, has given the Torah unto His people Israel.

Praised be the name of the Ruler of the universe, praised be the crown of Thy glory, the place where Thou thronest.

May Thy grace ever reign over Israel, that Thy saving hand may become manifest in Thy people, and in Thy Sanctuary;—that Thy heavenly light may descend upon us in its lustre, and our prayers be graciously accepted by Thee.

Thus, then, I stand before Thee, my God, ready to serve Thee, and bend my knee, now and always, before Thee and

Thy holy Law. I do not rely upon men, not upon them who imagine to be gods, do I put my trust, but I confide in Thee, upon God in heaven. Thou art the true God, Thy Law is truth, and Thy prophets are true. Thou bestowest blessings and doest wonders in truth. Upon Thee I rely, and in Thee I confide, and I praise and glorify Thy holy name by the emotions of my heart and the utterances of my lips! May it be Thy will to open my heart unto Thy divine precepts, and to fulfill the wishes of my heart unto me and Thy whole people Israel, that we may be remembered unto life, happiness and peace. Amen.

MEDITATION ON THE HOLY SABBATH.

Be welcome to me with thy soothing tranquillity, thou day of sober and joyous rest, for in thee germinate undisturbed the sacred blossoms of silent virtue; and the soul, removed from the tumult of the sensual world, readily listens to the lovely voice of religion. When, in the diverting bustle of life, my heart forgets the high purpose of human existence—when enticed by vanity, it strays from the path of the good—then, receive me, thou comforter, in thy holy shades; that in thy lap I may strengthen myself for the gladdening performance of my sacred duties. When I become weary on the rough road, on which secret passions cripple or paralyse the power to exercise good and noble deeds; when, with this weak feminine heart, which, alas, but too often is overcome by vanity, I feel ashamed how grievously I sinned against the Father of all: be thy sacred calmness, day of holy rest, my comforter and protector! But I also will never waste thy hallowed hours in senseless, indolent, mental vacancy, but ever devote them to the highest purposes attainable on earth, so that I may be elevated to that nobility of the mind which will draw me nearer to the Eternal, the ideal of all virtues, and which will easily raise me above all sorrows of the times. Then shall I be able to say with consoling confidence: I have, in letter and spirit, observed the divine commandment revealed on Sinai: —"remember the Sabbath day, to keep it holy," then shall I with assurance await that blessing which the All-merciful vouchsafed to all those who do not desecrate the Sabbath in any way, nor profane it by sanctioning any unholy work.

PRAYER FOR THE CLOSE OF THE SABBATH.

Almighty God, Rock of my salvation! in Thy name I conclude the day of rest and sanctification, and with it the week, during which Thou didst shower upon me the gifts of Thy loving-kindness, and didst provide me from the inexhaustible fountain of Thy paternal blessings with every thing that I needed for my support and the maintenance of those near and dear to my heart. My heart swells with gratitude towards Thee, my devotion is kindled and burns like a flame within me—Oh! would that my lips were able to express it. But Thou, O Lord! searchest the heart, examinest the thoughts of man, and acceptest the will for the deed, and even our aspiration towards virtue is accepted and counted by Thee for its practice. Yet, without Thine aid we cannot find the right path, nor fulfill our duties. Therefore, O God! I pray unto Thee, at the beginning of a new week, to which Thou hast preserved our lives, to open unto us the gates of understanding, of knowledge, and of enlightenment, that we may shun evil and sin, all that is immoral, useless and reprehensible, and enter, pure and sanctified, into the gates of virtue, piety and chastity! Open unto us the gates of contentment and tranquillity of the heart, and concord and peace, of universal unity and brotherly love, that we may envy no one, and no one may envy us. Open unto us the gates of blessing, of prosperity and happiness, that all the works of our hands may be crowned with success. Open unto us the gates of joy and delight, of acceptance and fulfillment, that we may behold the realization of the gladsome promise which Thou hast given unto the pious and righteous: "And the Lord shall give unto thee according to the desire of thy heart and prosper all thy designs. Thou shalt also decree a thing, and it shall be established unto thee, and the light shall shine upon thy ways." Amen.

PRAYER ON THE SABBATH PREVIOUS TO THE NEW MOON.

O God, Fountain of all happiness! another month will soon be carried in the swift stream of time to the endless host of its predecessors; and a new one will rise in its stead from the ocean of Eternity, which carries in its lap many a cheering, but also many a saddening fate. Therefore, do we appear before Thee, O Lord, to implore on this day Thy paternal blessing. Open, O Creator of time, the gates of mercy, and admit the prayer of a heart which, in humility and meekness, prostrates itself before Thee. Give me, O Father, what Thou deemest beneficial to me, and teach me to make the most sacred use of Thy gifts. Neither gold nor treasures, but cheerfulness and contentment, be my portion. Endow me with that firm belief in Thee which no affliction, no calamity, however dire, can shake. Bless me with a true unalloyed love, which is able to sacrifice a life for a friend, and to pardon the bitterest enemy. Send me, Creator of light, some cheering rays from Thy Throne of Light, that I may not lose my way, never wander from the straight road, but always adhere to the observance of

Thy laws, and render myself worthy of Thy love. Bless me with hope, to look forward with full confidence to yonder regions where my soul may find all again whom death hath taken away. Bless me with peace of mind and repose of the soul, with love of justice and truth, so that with the coming month I may find myself brought nearer to the goal, for which I have to prepare myself here on earth. Be Thou my support and my staff, that I may live before Thee a life of righeousness, and that I may at all times obey the faithful behests of Thine infinite wisdom. Amen

PRAYER FOR THE DAY OF NEW MOON.

Lord of life, who regulatest the course of time,—Thou hast divided it into great and small periods, into years, months, and days. This change of periods teaches us, how time rusheth hence in swift, uninterrupted flight and, with every onward movement, carries us nearer unto the end of all earthly existence, unto eternity; and that fleeting time, when once passed away, will never come back, despite all our wishes and ardent desires for its return. Therefore, we should employ it as long as we may yet call it ours, not waste even the least tittle thereof, lose no hour by idle sports or trifling, by useless deed and practice: for Thou, O Lord! wilt, on some future day, call us to account for every moment of our life!

Therefore, O Heavenly Father! I pray to Thee, for understanding and knowledge, that I may so employ my time, as to be for a blessing unto me and my dear ones, and unto my fellow-beings; that I may use every hour, every moment of my life unto wise activity and industry, unto successful labor and work,—for the ennoblement of my heart, for the preparation and cultivation of my soul, for eternity. O All-good Father, who hast thus far guided and shielded me, continue to grant Thy gracious protection unto me and mine; may the coming month be unto me a month of peace and joy,—preserve our health and lives, soften and lighten our grief,—increase our pleasure in life,—bless the works of our hands and our industry, and vouchsafe unto us, from the fullness of Thy grace, all that of which we may stand in need, and which may be beneficial to us—Amen.

FESTIVAL PRAYERS.

FOR THE FIRST DAYS OF PASSOVER

My God and Lord! the Festival of Passover has come, the joyful Feast of the memorial of the days of jubilee, when Thou didst redeem our forefathers from inhuman oppression, and didst carry them, with outstretched hand, into the beautiful land of liberty; from the dark abode of error and false belief, into the sunny realms of knowledge, and the pure, gladdening belief in Thee and Thy divine word, O my Heavenly Father.

With emotion and joy do we celebrate this Festival, which reminds us of that happy time, when Thou didst choose Israel for Thine inheritance, elect him from all nations, betroth him unto Thee as the bridegroom betrothes his bride, and bind him unto Thee with the ties of grace and love; and when Thy people, in return, clung unto Thee as a youthful bride to the heart of her beloved one, as a child to its mother's breast,—went after Thee, full of love and faithfulness, into a strange, unknown land, followed Thee into a dreary desert and wilderness. A long space of time has since then passed away,—the heart of Thy people has since then often changed, but Thy love has ever remained the same! *"Thou hast been a help and refuge unto our fathers from eternity, a shield and help unto their children after them, throughout all times."* Thou art our Guide, our Protector, our Guardian, as Thou hast been from all times.

We have passed through more than *one* Egypt. Hatred and prejudice laid a heavy yoke upon our necks—but through the darkness of misery and oppression a ray of Thy grace continually shone above us, and has at last brought on a morning of redemption, in which our human dignity is recognized and we live free and undisturbed under the protection of mild and just laws. Oh! mayest Thou, All-good Father, be further with us. As, in those days, Thou didst burst the chains in which our fathers sighed, and with an awful hand break the yoke of bondage and tyranny, so mayest Thou deliver and redeem our souls from the degrading yoke of sin and passion, that they may rise, with untrammeled, victorious power, above all attacks and temptations; and as Thou didst hurl from their altars the numberless idols and gods of Egypt, so may Thy boundless mercy assist us also, to subdue and destroy all the idols of vanity and worldly pleasure, that all our inner parts may be filled with Thee, Thou incomparable, exalted and glorious Being, thoroughly permeated by filial faithfulness and love,—by unshaken, unchangeable confidence and unbounded attachment to Thee, who art the Shield and Savior of every single being as well as of whole nations, and art nigh unto them with Thy help in trouble and suffering!

Thus, my God! mayest Thou cause Thy grace to reign over us, to exalt and sanctify us with Thy spirit. Blessed be Thou who sanctifiest Israel and the Festivals. Amen.

FOR THE LAST DAYS OF PASSOVER.

Almighty God! great and glorious were Thy works and miraculous Thy power wherewith Thou didst break the tyranny of Egypt and make our ancestors free; yet greater and more glorious was the help which Thou didst bestow upon them, when the mighty hosts of the pursuing enemy caused them again to tremble and despair on the shore of the Red Sea, where Thou didst deliver them from a twofold danger, that they could triumphantly exclaim: *"The Lord is my strength and song, and He is become my salvation; He is my God, and I will prepare Him a habitation; my fathers' God, and I will exalt Him."* Do Thou, my God! preserve within us the memory of these Thy glorious works, that we may never despair when dangers encompass us;—fill us with the consoling conviction, that Thou, with Thine outstretched arm, wilt lead us also through all the perils of the stormy ocean of this life,—that Thou wilt ever struggle for us, as long as we trust in Thy grace and loving-kindness.

Grant us, O God! strength and perseverance in our progress towards the promised land of light and truth; fill us with humility and forbearance in prosperity, and with confidence and resignation in adversity;—be Thou unto us a pillar of cloud in the days of happiness, that we may not become proud and overbearing and go astray, and a pillar of fire in the dark nights of misfortune, that we may never stumble or fall on our ways of life.

Accept, O Benign Father! our joyful thanks which on this festive day we offer up unto Thee for Thine infinite grace and goodness, wherewith Thou hast again removed from us reproach and ignominy, freed us from oppression and persecution, and caused us again to enjoy the blessings of a beloved home, where we may again live unto

Thee and our holy religion, unmolested and unharmed.—
Oh! implant in our hearts unshaken obedience to Thy
holy Law, that we may ever listen to the doctrines of virtue
and righteousness written therein; preserve within us
faithful reveration for Thy sacred precepts, that we may ever
well appreciate and worthily use our freedom, for the honor and glory of Thy holy name, and the name of Israel,
for the welfare of all men, for our own benefit here on
earth, and our salvation in life eternal. Amen.

FOR THE FEAST OF WEEKS.—(PENTECOST.)

With the most profound reverence, O Lord! do we, this
day, proclaim Thy glory and praise Thee for the infinite grace
which Thou didst manifest on Sinai unto our forefathers,
unto us, and unto all Thy beings created in Thine eternal
image. Our hearts rejoice, our souls exalt at the memory
of that day on which Thy majesty appeared, in the fullness
of its lustre, upon the sacred mountain, to reveal the law
of life unto Thy people And this people are we. Thou
didst call us from out of all nations to be Thine inheritance,
the priests of Thy Law, the messengers of salvation unto
all the families of the earth. Oh! how great is Thy grace,
O God ! how inexhaustible Thy loving-kindness. From the
beginning Thou hast placed man high upon the pinnacle
of creation. Endowed with the light of reason and far
surpassing all other visible beings, he was destined to raise
his eye to Thee, to seek and find Thee in Thy wonderful
works. But soon his eye grew dark,—the fetters of wordly
sense pinioned the wings of his spirit. Instead of soaring
from the visible creatures to the Invisible Creator, he sank
into the dust before finite beings and called created beings,
which Thou, O God! hadst placed far below him, his gods!
And thus plunged in error and delusion, thus blinded, men

could no longer read even the holy law of morality which Thou hast engraven, with indelible characters, upon the tablets of our hearts, and they practised the most abominable vices for the worship of their idol gods. The earth was filled with, and defiled by all kind of abominations; lust and murder were deemed pious deeds, and the human race seemed to be irretrievably delivered up unto perdition. Then, O Father! didst Thou appear on Mount Sinai, with the flaming Law in Thy right hand,—and upon Thy mighty command, light and darkness, Israel and the nations were separated from each other. A small tribe was commissioned, by Thine inscrutable counsel, to become a dam against the torrent of corruption, a pattern and guardian-angel unto all mankind;—Israel's doctrines, example and destiny should give testimony of Thee, the One in Unity, and, on some future day, lead all the children of the earth unto Thy worship and glorification, to make all of them Thy people. Were we possessed even of angel tongues, we could, nevertheless, not sufficiently thank Thee for the sublime mission which Thou hast imposed upon us,—for Thine endless mercy wherewith Thou hast safely carried us through the all-swallowing stream of time. Years, numerous as the sand on the sea-shore, have passed before us, and even to this day we do firmly cling to our priestly office;—even to this day Thy word is our light, our life, our joy;—even to this day we do wait, with unshaken trust, upon the fulfillment of Thy promise unto our forefather Abraham: "*Thy seed shall be as numberless as the stars of heaven, a blessing unto all the families of the earth.*" O God! grant, that that promised time may soon come. Do Thou reveal Thy glory unto all the world, as Thou didst once reveal it on Mount Sinai unto Thy people Israel! establish everywhere the reign of light, truth and virtue, that they may rule over darkness, error and malice,—that the great day may come, on which all nations shall go up to Thy holy mountain,—when Thy house shall be called a house of prayer unto all nations, and from one end of the world even unto the other thereof the exulting shout shall be heard: "Zion, thy God reigneth, now and for ever more!" Amen.

MEDITATION ON THE DECALOGUE.

With holy emotions do I greet this festive day, this cradle-feast of our sublime Religion, this memorial of that grand season, which brought so much salvation and blessing into this world.

Amidst the roar of thunder and flashes of lightning, Thou, O Father of All, didst descend upon the modest brow of Sinai and didst speak unto Thy people in Thy sublime, yet tender, language;—Thou, the High and Exalted One, camest down to the weak, finite son of man to reveal Thyself unto him in Thy glory and majesty, and give him statutes of justice and truth, doctrines of comfort and elevation.

Unto the joyful event of this Festival we are indebted for our highest treasure, our most costly jewel—the *Ten Commandments*, these pillars and corner stones of our quickening faith, these faithful guides and leaders through life pointing out the paths of right and duty,—these props and saving anchors in woe and trouble, containing all that elevates the spirit, ennobles the heart, renders man more human and children more childlike, and affords consolation to the despairing and confidence unto the doubting.

1. "I am the Eternal thy God who have brought thee out of the land of Egypt, from the house of bondage."

This is the first word of Divine Revelation.

Oh! be blessed unto me, thou glorious word! That

which the presentiment of the heart proclaims unto us with a small, still voice, Thou callest unto the world with loud tones,—That which is inscribed upon every page of the Book of Nature, Thou providest with Thy seal and endorsement: *There is a God!* A God of supreme power, who with a mighty arm crushed our oppressors and persecutors,—a God of compassion, who lendeth His ear unto the lamentations of the oppressed and enthralled, who breaketh all bars and fetters to lead them unto liberty and happiness. Oh! how my heart does widen with joy and confidence in Him, who with infinite love extendeth His hand unto me also, whenever woe and oppression encompass me, whenever the hand of persecution is heavily laid upon me, whenever the gates of happiness are closed before me.

2. "Thou shalt have no other gods before me."

The Eternal is One, Sole God, unto Him alone belong all glory, praise and adoration; unto Him, thou heart of mine, dedicate thy worship, thy love, thy thankfulness! It is He alone who graciously leads me through life,—my Creator and Savior, who guides my youth, protects mine old age, who is always and everywhere the same, in the heavens above, and on the earth below, and in the depth of the ocean. Therefore, be of good cheer and courage, my soul! Even though thy destiny may not be smiling, even though grief and pain may depress thee, bear it all with patience and resignation, hopefully and trustfully, for He, the All-wise and All-loving Father, our Sole Guardian and Ruler, who in His wisdom creates the storm as well as sunshine, has thus ordained it for thee, and whatever He does cannot be but for our salvation. He will make all things right.

3. "Thou shalt not utter the name of the Eternal unto falsehood."

How should we utter the name of Him whose whole being is truth and faithfulness unto untruth? Faitfulness and sincerity are rays of His divine being, they ennoble the heart which receives them, and elevate it unto the likeness of the Eternal. Oh! may these god-like feelings never depart from my heart,—may they ever dwell upon my lips, that the thoughts of my soul, as well as the words of my mouth may find favor, in Thy preence my God, and Lord.

4. "Six days shalt thou labor and do all thy work; but the seventh day is a day of rest."

If idleness is a pernicious vice, continual hunting after earthly possessions, unceasing cares and anxieties, efforts and exertions for worldly acquisitions and aspirations are no less fatal and destructive. Our body would grow weary, our spirit, soon forgetting its heavenly mission upon earth, would sacrifice its heavenly treasures for earthly gifts, if God, in His provident grace, had not appointed the Sabbath for us, that we may thereon refresh our bodies and direct our minds towards the contemplation of all that is divine. On that day, all shall participate in quickening repose, parents and children, masters and servants; even the brute creation has been included by All-loving God in this command concerning the Sabbath. "God *blessed* the Sabbath-day and *hallowed* it;" and it will become a *blessing* unto us, if we *sanctify* ourselves on it and through it by ennobling meditations, by communion with our Protector and Creator.

5. "Honor thy father and mother."

Our ancient Sages remark: Three beings have a share in man: *God, his father, and his mother!* How sublime and sacred must filial duty appear in the eyes of God, for He calls for its performance by a threefold voice : by the feeling of filial love inmate in our very being;—by the law of thankfulness towards our parents who are our guardian angels on earth and have, after God, the gratest share in our being;—and lastly by the divine command: "Honor thy father and thy mother, that it may be well with thee." Thus, then, be thrice hallowed unto me, thou sweet duty! My father and mother,—Oh! how my heart throbs for you in love and gratitude;—I will use all my power to fulfill the divine command of filial reverence resounding from all the chords of my soul.

6. "Thou shalt not murder."

The life of our neighbor must be unto us a sacred, inviolable good. But not his life alone, but all that beautifies and cheers his life, must not be violated or endangered by us. It does not always require a sword or dagger to strike the heart of man; an insidious, slanderous word often turns into a poisonous arrow, that strikes as deep wounds and causes death. Spiritual murder is not less destructive than a deathblow struck by a murderer's hand, nor less punishable in the eyes of God.

7. "Thou shalt not commit adultery."

The most sacred treasure, the most priceless boon for wedded people are matrimonial love and faithfulness. Who would with ruthless hand destroy this crown, rend this wreath,—who with wicked levity trample upon these tender blossoms that ornament the matrimonial Eden ? Before the gates of this Eden, God, in His grace, has placed, as a Cherub with a flaming sword, His divine command: "Thou shalt not commit adultery!" in order that every careless thought, every sinful emotion be frightened off and recoil in fear and trembling.

8. "Thou shalt not steal."

Let the thought never enter Thy mind to appropiate the property of thy neighbor to thyself. Whether he may have acquired his possessions by his own industry, whether God's blessing alone, without his own co-operation, may have made him rich, do never resolve to lay thy hand thereon. Theft—whatever form or name it may assume: violence, fraud, or cunning—is at all times the same. In whatever way thou mayest deprive thy neighbor of his own, it will never turn unto thy salvation,—the blessing of God will flee from thee. Thou hast defiled thy hand with the most vulgar, the basest deed, and God, the Pure, the Just, the Exalted One, will in His anger turn His countenance from thee.

9. "Thou shalt not bear false witness."

How much calamity and evil do we cause in this world by false testimony! Though we do not perpetrate a crime with our own hand, yet we sustain it by false testimony in court, and often, by means of a word, lead vice unto victory and triumph,—mislead judges to unjust decisions,—oppress innocence, which will cry unto God for revenge against us. Perchance we may think, that the wrong which we favor may not be very great, may be very excusable; but who can ever measure the range that sin may take? Evil must beget evil, injustice must produce injustice. Whenever we have once extended our hand to sin, it extends itself, ere we are aware thereof, increases in dimension, immeshes us in its destructive net, that we can never escape, and behold, to our horror, that we are given up a prey to its power.

10. "Thou shalt not covet anything that is thy neighbor's."

O envy, thou source of all vices! Whatever we possess as

our own, whatever the grace of God has vouchsafed unto us, thou makest appear little and insignificant in our eyes; only that which belongs unto our neighbor thou presentest in lustre and beauty,—after it thou directest our wishes, incitest our desires. Thou dost robb our heart of its peace, turnest our life into a torment; from the heaven of a contented mind thou hurlest us into the depths of discontent and discord with ourselves. Therefore, will I guard myself against envy, against covetousness of what belong unto others and that which God has deemed well to deny me.

Praise be unto Thee, O Heavenly Father, for these divine, gladdening and saving doctrines and ordinances. They are unto us a priceless gift of Thy grace and truth, my God, we will bear them within our hearts, fasten them at the door-post of our houses, bind them upon our hands and foreheads, that they may ever remain before our eyes, and guide us in our lives,—that their light may open our eyes unto truth, their admonitions strengthen us in the performance of our duties, and, by pointing to Thee, Thou Exalted One, cause us to find peace and consolation, so as to enable us cheerfully and courageously to enter upon the contest with the troubles and cares of earthly life.

Grant, O God, that the celebration of this Festival may consecrate my whole life, may make it a great festive day,—a feast of commemoration of Thy holy Law, of Thy divine *Ten Words*. Amen.

PRAYER FOR THE ANNIVERSARY OF THE DESTRUCTION OF THE TEMPLE (תשעה באב).

With profound fervor, O Lord! do we this day remember the fatal day on which the enemy entered Thy fortress, and Thy Sanctuary became a prey unto consuming flames. — "How the city sat solitary that was full of people, — the princess among the provinces, a mourning widow." Israel's pride and crown, the glorious Temple upon Moriah's proud heights wherein the children of Abraham praised the glory of Thy name *before* all nations,—the lustrous abode of the Ark with the divine testimony and the Cherubim pair with their heavenward turned wings,—the altar with the atoning sacrifice, the candelstick with its seven tongues of fire—: all sank into ruins;—the sweet song of the Levites that had risen up to Thee in thousand voices was hushed, and the wails of the Priests robbed of their ministrations and dignity, the cries and lamentations of the children of Thy people deprived of their houses, were alone heard. Alas! heavy and bitter affliction didst Thou impose upon the house of Jacob on that day! With bleeding hearts did the poor pilgrims tear themselves away from their dearly beloved house of their youth, which had offered them so many gifts of imperishable salvation, such rich treasures of never-dying reminiscences, and started for a loveless strange land, like children whom their father had rejected, everywhere surrounded by raving cries of hostile nations, everywhere nurtured with sufferings, wrapt in the garb of slaves, beaten and wounded unto death, that they often cried unto Thee from out of their misery: "Thou hast laid me in the lowest pits, in darkness, in the deeps; Thy wrath lieth hard upon me, and Thou hast afflicted me with all Thy waves; Thou hast taken away all my friends far from me, and hast made me an abomination unto them; I am shut up, and I cannot come forth; mine eye grows blind from grief, Lord! I call upon Thee, the whole day I stretch out my hands unto Thee; wilt Thou shew wonders unto the dead,—can shadows rise again? Why, O God, castest Thou off my soul, why hidest Thou Thy face from me? Thy fierce wrath goeth over me, Thy terrors surround me; lover and friend hast Thou taken from me, and darkness is mine acquaintance!"

Yea, unutterable woe hath Israel suffered during the numberless days of his pilgrimage! his shoulder whereon the government once lay, became a path for wanderers; his eye, once shining with the brilliancy of happines, became an inexhaustible fountain of tears. Where'er his fugitive foot trod, he found the yoke of oppression, the curse of hatred, the poisonous arrow of calumny, and many thousands of his sons and daughters were compelled to sacrifice their fortunes and lives in their struggles for Thee and Thy holy Law; yet they were more fleeting than an eagle, stronger than a lion in the performance of Thy sublime will,—inseparable, both in life and in death, from their faithfulness unto Thee, Thou Unsearchable One, who createst the pure from impure, light from darkness, and wilt lead also Thy people from the deepest ignominy of degradation unto the most glorious goal, unto the most beautiful triumph. And this elevating thought affords us also consolation, courage and hope, aye! it changes our mourning into joy, our lamentation into cries of exultation. However deeply and sorely our soul may be affected by the memory of the unutterable woe wherewith our ancestors went forth from their own Zion into the vast wilderness of heathen nations, however great our pain may be at the contemplation of the long journey of heavy sufferings and great sacrifices which our race has since had to pass:—in all these bitter trials we recognize Thy loving paternal guidance, a means towards the fulfillment of Thine infallible promises, towards the glorification of Thy name and of Thy law, before the eyes of all nations. No! not as a rejected son did Thy first-born go forth into a strange land, but as Thy messenger unto all the families of the earth. Israel should no longer dwell solitary and separate from Thy other children who were languishing in night and darkness, but carry his blessings everywhere like a fertilizing stream. The One Temple of God at Jerusalem sank into ruins, in order that numberless Temples might rise all over the earth unto Thy honor and glory. The ancient priestly dignity and sacrificial service vanished, in order that the whole Congregation of Israel, in accordance with its original mission, may become a ministering priest, and every member thereof may offer sacrifices wherewith Thou wilt be more pleased than with the blood of animals and thousands of rivers of oil,—sacrifices of practical charity, love for God and man,—sacrifices of a pure and holy life, which will not deviate from the path of truth even in suffering and death,—sacrifices of that unprecedented faithfulness to God, whose miracles are attested by the history of thousands of years. Thine imperishable testimony has remained inviolate and has risen purified and with heightened lustre from that bitterly bewailed conflagration, relieved from walls which had become for it a dungeon and shut out its glory from the view of millions of beings standing without, created in Thine image and intended to be elevated by Thy Priest, to be Thy people. From the flames that consumed Zion, the Messiah was born, suffering Israel, who, relieved from the bonds of childhood, proceeds through the world, a man of sorrows, without form and comeliness, despised and rejected, that with his chains he may lead his own tormentors unto freedom, through his wounds carry healing unto them that had smitten him, in order that,—after his soul had made an offering for sin—he should behold seed, happily accomplish God's will, and be rejoiced and satisfied by the sight of the numberless hosts that will come to join him from all parts.

Thus, then, O Lord! this day has turned, according to the proclamation of Thy prophet, from a day of fast and mourning into a feast of joy, when we remember the glorious development of Thy Law, and our sublime Messianic mission which commenced with the event commemorated on this day. Though this sublime mission has cost us bitter sacrifices, and though the way which we have still to pass is long:—our hearts are full of gratitude for the infinite grace which Thou hast vouchsafed unto us, to be the ministering priests for all mankind; and our confidence in Thy promise shall never be shaken, that all that hath breath shall on some future day bow before Thee. Grant, O God, that all Israel may know the goal of their pilgrimage and pursue it with united energy and cheerful courage! Grant, that their mourning may end everywhere, where'er they may yet sigh under the yoke of hatred; open the eyes of all those who still regard Thy messenger as rejected from before Thy countenance, and limit the house of the world-conquering Prince of God to that narrow spot whereon his cradle stood in ancient time!

Mayest Thou, then, strengthen us all in Thy service, fortify us for our mission, and cause us soon to enter upon that promised time, when the vast earth shall be an altar for trespass-offerings, whereon all spirits and hearts will rise to Thee with burning love,—when the Doctrine of Truth and the Law of life's sanctification shall, as protecting Cherubim, expand their wings over the Sanctuary of a race lovingly united among themselves and with Thee;—when all mankind shall shine in the same lustre, like that candlestick which was made of one piece of pure gold, and sent forth from seven arms its brilliant light;—when that Temple shall rise which Thine own hand shall build out of the same fire which destroyed that made by human hands,—out of the heavenly fire, from which Thou didst reveal Thyself on Sinai unto the people of Israel, and on Zion unto all Thy children, that Thy promise may be fulfilled of a new Jerusalem which Thou wilt surround as with a wall of flames. Amen.

PRAYER FOR THE MONTH OF ELLUL.

This concluding month of the year is full of serious and sublime significance for us: for in these last days of the departing year our souls should prepare themselves for that great day, on which Thou wilt sit in judgment over us,—Thou, the Most Holy One, over us frail, sinful human beings, Thou, before whom even the inhabitants of heaven can not appear sufficiently pure,—how much less we with our weak, vacillating heart which is so often led astray by the allurements and temptations of this earth, into which sin enters through our eyes and ears to occupy a lasting abode, and which consciously or unconsciously, often deviates from Thee and violates Thy holy laws.

Consecrated and sanctified unto us are these days, on which, in our prayers and petitions, we implore Thy pardon and forgiveness, O All-merciful God! for our sins, on which we are anxious to wash away, by our repentance and tears, the blots and stains of guilt. We long to return unto Thee with true, sincere hearts, and with the firm resolution to mend our ways and practices.

Oh! do Thou sanctify unto us these days through Thy blessings and grace. All-merciful God! grant that they may become for us days of return, and reconciliation with Thee, O Heavenly Father!—days of true improvement and sanctification, on which our hearts may be filled with renewed love for virtue and religion; on which the quickening spirit of justice and peace may enter our souls, and we may feel ourselves impelled by its beatific influence to good and noble deeds, strengthened for the struggle against weakness and sin;—that these days may become for us days of hearing and fulfilling our prayers and petitions, days of pardon and forgiveness of all our iniquities before Thee, our Lord. Amen.

FOR THE EVE OF NEW YEAR.

Almighty God!
"*In olden times didst Thou lay the foundation of the earth; and the heavens are the works of Thy hands. These will indeed perish, but Thou wilt ever exist: yea, all of them will wear out like a garment; as a vesture wilt Thou change them, and they will be changed; but Thou art ever the same, and Thy years will have no end.*"

With this exclamation of the inspired Psalmist do we draw nigh unto Thee, in this first hour of the solemn Festival of Memorial and New-Year, and most humbly bow down before Thee, O King and Ruler of the Universe! to acknowledge the eternity and unchangeableness of Thy being, and remember Thine infinite justice and loving kindness wherewith Thou mindest and preservest Thy numberless creatures, and hast again granted us to live unto the beginning of another year, to enter upon a new period of life, and to continue afresh the working out of our sublime destination upon earth.

When we cast an examining glance at the past year, we perceive that,—tho' it is but a short space of time which hath vanished away like a dream,—it is well apt to fill our hearts with manifold emotions, and our souls with serious and solemn reflections. Bitter grief mingles with profound joy within our bosoms, while we most thankfully remember Thy paternal guidance which Thou hast so often manifested unto us during the past year.

We thank Thee, O All-good Father, for the manifold blessings and benefits, which Thou hast bestowed upon us,—for food and raiment,—for the preservation of health and life, for Thine ever-ready protection against danger and temptation.—We praise Thee, O God! for all the blessings which Thou hast vouchsafed unto all those endeared to our hearts, and whose lives are wedded unto ours by the ties of blood, love, friendship, and noble purposes.

With calm resignation and profound confidence in Thy holy will, we bow down before Thine inscrutable wisdom and justice, and piously submit to the trials and afflictions wherewith Thou didst deem it fit to visit us. For unto Thee alone it is known, why we must suffer, why the cup of life is so often filled with bitter draughts; and it behooves us, therefore, to accept *them* also with the pious and consoling conviction, that Thou sendest grief and sorrow for our own welfare and salvation. Oh! accept the tears of woe and pain for those dear to us, whom Thou hast removed from us, henceforth to dwell with Thee in the realms of everlasting bliss and peace, where we shall meet them again, never to be separated!

All-merciful Lord! Transient and fleeting is this earthly pilgrimage; Oh! may we ever be mindful thereof, that pride and vanity may never enter our hearts, and charity and love actuate us in all our sentiments, words and deeds. Oh! may we always remember, that this life is but a shadow, and ourselves, like the flowers of the fields which bloom but a short while soon to wither and die, and that we, therefore, may never neglect with holy avarice to use the time, and conscientiously prepare ourselves, during this short existence of ours, for eternity and its blessings and treasures. May we never forget, that Thou hast kindled within us a light from Thine eternal spirit, never to die, but to elevate us above all other creatures, to enable us to look up to Thee, to adore Thee, and to comprehend that Thou hast not placed us here on earth to live for a few years, and then to sink down into eternal night and destruction, but to make us partakers of eternal life and salvation. Do Thou enlighten us with a ray of Thy wisdom, that we may ever choose right from wrong, good from evil, exercise justice and mercy towards all our fellow-beings, walk humbly before Thee, and thus create and promote peace and concord among all mankind. Oh! do Thou fortify us against all error and temptation,—and whenever sin should have led us astray, lead us back upon the path of piety and rectitude.

Father of all mercies! give us also during the coming year *"bread to eat and raiment to put on,"* but above all, peace of mind and contentment of the heart; protect us against adversity and bitter grief. Preserve us all, that we may inspire each other to noble deeds, and work together for our own sanctification, the glory of Thy holy name, and the honor of our sacred Religion.

All-bounteous God! *"Be not angry with me, now that I have taken upon me to speak unto my Lord, although I am but dust and ashes."* I cannot yet leave Thee ere I have recommended unto Thy paternal care the widows and the orphans, the weak and the poor, the afflicted and the mourning. Oh! pour Thy heavenly balm upon the wounded, grant Thy stay and staff to the falling and oppressed, and Thy protection to the forsaken and persecuted. Oh! do not withdraw Thyself from those that are prostrated upon the bed of sickness, and awaken for them tender and pious souls to alleviate their sufferings.—And whomsoever Thou shouldst summon hence, to-day or to-morrow, let his breaking eye behold Thy countenance, that his departure from those dear to his heart may be easy, and that he may go hence with the strengthening belief, That Thou wilt receive us all in grace and in mercy upon Thy holy mountain.

Oh! may this new year become unto all whom my lips have named before Thee, and unto those whom I have not mentioned, a year of bliss, peace and salvation! May it bring unto us new life, new strength, and new hopes, that we may joyfully continue our earthly pilgrimage, until it be concluded and we depart hence to celebrate that New Year which shall never grow old, but last unto all eternity. Amen.

FOR THE NEW YEAR'S DAY.

Almighty God! as we concluded the old year before Thee, with tears and prayers, thus we assemble again in the first hours of the new, in Thy Sanctuary, to dedicate unto Thee our emotions, and open our hearts before Thy paternal eyes.

O God! how many are the things to be implored of Thee for the new year. As a child approaches its father, so do we open unto Thee our hearts and souls, confide unto Thee our joys and sorrows, our thoughts and feelings. Whatever secret woe may depress us, whatever our souls may hesitate to place upon our lips, the glowing tears of our eyes utter before Thee this day, our sighs and weeping lay bare before Thee.

But above all it is this that moves our souls: we know this is the day of memorial, to-day the year past steps before Thee with our deeds and works, to testify *for* or *against* us. With fear and trembling do we look back upon it,—with alarm do we ask ourselves: what shall the past year testify concerning us? Did we employ it for good and blissful works? Have we used the day; thereof unto our eternal salvation, unto our ennoblement and improvement, or did we carelessly waste them in labors of vanity, merely to enjoy the fleeting fruits of life? Or did they vanish hence like a dream, disappear like a cloud without value and importance, without gain and profit?—The year is irretrievably gone, but the work of man, both good and evil, which he performed, has remained, and the memory of our shortcomings weighs heavily upon our souls, pierces our hearts with sharp stings, covers us with shame and disgrace! Only profoundly confiding in Thine endless grace and mercy we draw nigh unto Thee, this day, in order to expiate, with our sighs and tears, the heavy guilt beneath which we are sighing. Thy compassion and loving-kindness alone, which do not desire the death of the sinner, but that he may return and live, are my hope and consolation. With humility and contrition I call upon Thy holy name, exclaiming: Forgive, Father of all men, forgive my sins and deal with me according to the measure of Thy mercy which is great, and not according my guiltiness. Mayest Thou guard and protect me in the new year as Thou hast done heretofore; preserve all those dear to me, inscribe us in the book of life unto life, unto happiness, unto welfare: avert from us all evil accident, all sad destiny; cause the fruit of life to ripen unto us with mildness and sweetness. Cause the sun of Thy grace to illumine our paths, vouchsafe the fullness of Thy divine blessing unto all our works, success unto all our endeavors, salvation unto all our labors, realization unto all our hopes, and fulfillment unto all our wishes. Truly and lastingly bind around us the blissful tie of peace and concord. Cause Thy compassion to behold all our grief, and send healing unto all the pains and wounds of our souls, as unto the ills and diseases of our bodies; send Thy help and consolation unto all who may be in need thereof. Grant that we may patiently and resignedly submit to all situations of life, courageously and confidently look towards the future, and walk before Thee with pure hearts, until, at the close of our days of life, we shall appear before Thy heavenly throne to render our account of them. Amen.

MEDITATION FOR NEW YEAR'S DAY AND THE DAY OF ATONEMENT.

My God! how terrible and detestable is sin! Pure hast thou created the soul and breathed it into us,—but sin creeps around it as a poisonous plant that deprives a tree of its nourishment, and desecrates the child of heaven and disfigures in it the sublime image of its creator; sin settles in our heart, and extinguishes therein the divine ray, destroys every germ of goodness, it rises as a powerful barrier between the desecrated creature and the holy, high-exalted Deity;—it robs us of the sweet comforts of belief, and prevents us from looking up to Thee, my God;—it destroys our cheerfulness, and the peace and tranquillity of our minds, it darkens the heaven within us, covers us with shame and disgrace, and fills us with pain and woe.

Yea, terrible and detestable is sin, for it disfigures and destroys not only our mental being, it disfigures and destroys also our bodies. In return for that we allowed it to enter our inner parts, it shakes the pillars of our health, consumes the vigor and bloom of life, extinguishes from our countenances thy ray and reflection of our

God-likeness, whose impress innocence and purity of the heart have stamped upon them.

Oh! I abhor and abominate sin—I will shake it from me with all the strength of my soul! Awake within me, all ye aspirations unto good, and ye inclinations of my better being, to struggle against the power of evil within me;—awaken, O my conscience, in all thy strength, raise thine admonishing, threatening voice whenever the fascinating words of temptation reach my ear and I am in danger to be allured and infatuated by them! O my soul! remember thy sublime destination and tear thyself away from all connection with sin, control all sinful inclinations and habits, and be impressed of thy greatness, of thine elevated position above all that is base and vulgar; remember thy sublime worth and unite only with all that is sublime and worthy,—entertain only pure, chaste thoughts, only God-pleasing emotions, receive only such impressions as are not in conflict with the thought of God; devote thyself only to *such* wishes and aspirations as will not offend the conscience, as will not disturb thy peace and cheerfulness.

In these sacred hours which Thou, O God, hast set apart for our purification and atonement, for our return to virtue, for the communion of our spirits with all that is heavenly and divine—in these sacred hours I will unite all the energies of my being, all the feelings of my heart, all my wishes, all my aspirations and capacities in the *one* firm thought, in the *one* unshaken resolve: to destroy all evil inclinations and sinful desires within me, in order to effect a perfect improvement and conversion, a rebirth of the innocence and purity of my heart.

But, my God and Father! will the inspiration glowing

within me in these sacred halls, where I feel Thy presence more than in any other place,—will the enthusiasm that permeates me to-day on which mine ears are closed to all worldly utterances, on which I am severed and separated from all my relations with the world of vanity and its allurements, on which I am entirely absorbed in the contemplation of Thine high-exalted Being and mine own estate: will that enthusiasm and inspiration remain vivid within me, when I shall leave this sanctuary to return to the life and tumult of the world without, whenever I shall have to contend against *passions*, against *want* and sorrow,—when the infatuating voice of temptation shall resound in my ear, or whenever sin shall appear before me in the dazzling form of fame and honor?

Oh! conscious of the weakness and foibles of the human heart I tremble and fear that my pious intentions may again be shaken, that I may then turn faithless to my vows and resolutions! Grant, O All-merciful One! that the elevated influences of this solemn day may never be lost, that the spirit of righteousness which permeates me this day, may never depart from me. Grant, that sin, in whatever form and under whatever garb it may appear, may be hideous and abhorrent in mine eye, and that, however tempting its alluring flatteries may appear to my senses, I may, yet, never cease to hate it and flee from it; that I may ever honor what is truly good, acknowledge virtue in its exalted worth, in its everlasting sublimity; that I may ever love and distinguish it whenever and wherever I may meet it, even in the hut of poverty and misery, even in the garment of want and howliness! Oh! may I succeed ever to remain strong, firm and unshaken in all good and noble endeavors; may I become better and more and more like unto Thee, my God and Lord, that I may ever be able to look up to Thee with a clear conscience and cheerful confidence. Amen.

FOR THE EVE OF THE DAY OF ATONEMENT. (כל נדרי)

Lord, God! All-merciful, gracious, of abundant goodness and truth, forgiving iniquity, transgression and sins, I also have sinned, I feel my wrong and my guiltiness, and desire and seek of Thee mercy and forgiveness. Thou art a God of mercy, but also a God of justice, before whom there is neither hypocrisy, nor bribery, nor regard of person. How can I hope to be declared not guilty by Thee, when I know myself that I have sinned? But as I confess and repent my sins, renounce all inclinations unto evil, aspire after virtue and piety, and indeed amend my ways, so wilt Thou also in mercy look down upon me,—so will I become worthier of Thy grace and blessings, more susceptible of the influence of Thy spirit and Thy power,—and thus I shall return my natural relation with Thee and again enjoy its happiness. Thus it is said: *"The tenth day of this seventh month is the day of atonement, a holy convocation shall it be unto you, and a fast-day; on it no manner of work shall ye do, for it is a day of atonement, to make an atonement for you, before the Lord your God, a Sabbath-rest it shall be unto you, and ye shall fast: on the ninth day of the month at evening shall ye begin, from evening unto evening shall ye celebrate your Sabbath."* Thus the promise of Thy forgiveness is held out to us, of Thine everlasting, unchangeable will to pardon repentant and improving sinners. This promise affords confidence and joy to every one who is on the way of improvement. Feeling our weakness and foibles we may confidently approach Thee and trust in Thee as an indulgent, kind Father, as soon as we follow Thine admonition and indeed forsake the path of sin.—But when we draw nigh unto thee, confiding in the never-dying fountain of Thy love, we must first banish all hatred and vindictiveness from our hearts; when we call unto Thee as our father, we must first have shown ourselves as brothers towards our fellow-men: for the Day of Atonement can effect its work only then, after we have conciliated our brothers and sisters whom we may have offended or injured in the course of the past year, whose honor or property we may have violated. For thus it is said in Holy Writ: "*For on that day an atonement shall be made for you, to cleanse you: from all your sins before the Lord shall ye be clean.*" The day of Atonement works forgiveness for sins against the Eternal; but not for such committed against our fellow-men, so long as we have not satisfied them.

Thanks be unto Thee, O all-merciful Father, for the blissful revelations of Thy grace, for these consoling and indispensable assurances of Thy paternal love! How much is the work of improvement facilitated! We know certainly that Thou forgivest sins and remittest punishment and hast mercy as a father upon them who return to their duty and strive to please Thee; and Thou demandest of them neither sacrifices nor trespass-offerings, but only sincerity and truth. Thus it is said: "*Sacrifice and offerings Thou dost not desire, mine ears hast Thou opened,*"—"*Obedience is better than sacrifice,*"—now we know certainly, that it is not in vain to mend our ways, that it is pleasing unto Thee when we change our desires and ways, that Thou dost assist and strengthen us, and that Thou requirest no improvement of us which would go beyond our powers. And though we cannot expect that the evils naturally resulting from our sins and follies should be speedily removed as by a miracle, yet we hope that Thy supreme wisdom will turn all unto our own benefit. I will bear all ills which I have brought upon me by mine own aberrations, and Thou, O God, wilt turn them unto good for me and, sooner or later, convert them into sources of joy and gladness. Grant me strength, O Lord, to dedicate myself, according to Thy law, unto Thy service from evening even unto evening;—let not my body become weak, nor my spirit weary, that on to-morrow evening I may depart from this sacred place with the consolatory hope, that my prayer has been pleasing in Thy sight, and my actions shall ever be acceptable before Thy face, O Lord, my God. Amen.

FOR THE DAY OF ATONEMENT.

Almighty God! My heart trembles beneath Thine examining and all-penetrating eye; for I feel how far I have remained behind the fulfillment of my duties, how often I have sinned within my heart against my better inclinations, against Thy holy Law; how often even mine actions were prompted by sinister and impure motives,—how much, alas! how much still remains for me to do, and which my conscience would often and seriously urge me to accomplish! But now, in this sacred place, and on this holiest of days, mine ear does more distinctly and powerfully hear the rustling and rushing of Thine ever-present majesty, the thick veil sinks from before mine eyes, and with astonishment do I behold the shadowyness, the vanity and emptiness of all my intentions and aspirations, of all my toils and labors. Thine endless grace has endowed me with a breath from Thy breath, with a spirit from Thy spirit,—an angel, whom Thou hast crowned with honor and glory, whom Thou hast vested with the power of ruling over all living beings as well as the human body, called unto Thy service but for a short while,—an angel, whom Thou hast given unto me for a guardian and watchman, continually to teach me Thy name and Thy will, and successfully to lead me towards the place which Thou hast prepared for me, to guide me into the Sanctuary shining with unspeakable lustre, which Thy hand has established for an everlasting dwelling place, an abode of never ending beatitude unto all Thy worshippers. But sinfully reversing Thine all-wise ordination, 1 would bind that angel into the yoke of worldly, base desires,—made the ruler a slave, and the servant a ruler, aye! a tyrant! The gratification of my earthly wants and desires, the ingathering of harvests of dust and evanescence, and not instruction in Thy holy Law, nor the acquisition of holy, imperishable treasures, nor the knowledge of Thy name and will, nor pious meditation upon Thy Being and my destination beyond the grave, would I regard as the chief end of my labors, as the very object of life. I would hunt after earthly enjoyments with all the power of my soul,—to *them* I devoted all my thoughts, aspirations and actions, from the beginning of the year to the end thereof, by day and by night, when I laid me down and when I rose up. The hours which I dedicated unto Thee and Thy holy word, the moments during which my God-born spirit remembered its exalted dignity and mission,—these moments—O shame and disgrace!—appeared to me *lost,* because they were offered unto Thee and not unto my idols; aye! I would even go so far in my blind aberration to regret the loss of these moments, and call myself foolish because I interrupted my folly but for a few moments.——And yet, what would I be without Thee, Thou Unsearchable One? Thine is all, all that I am and possess. Thine eye would watch over me even before my birth and to this day; Thy hand has directed my steps, has safely carried me through numberless dangers,— Thou hast never ceased to cheer and gladden me. How could I number the benefits of which every day, every hour of my life has been full, from my earliest childhood, even to this moment? And though Thou wouldst visit me with bitter sorrows and heavy cares, mine own shortsighted eye would after all discover that they contained a germ of salvation,— that lamentation would change into joy,—that the tears I wept were seeds from which bliss and pleasure sprang forth. But how did I thank Thee for Thy merciful guidance? Whenever Thou didst vouchsafe abundant blessings upon me,—whenever Thou didst fulfill even the most glowing and boldest wishes of my heart, I would not praise Thee, but *myself;* I would soon forget the pious vows which I had promised unto Thee in the hours of grief and trouble, and would glory in mine own wisdom, strength and energy; I would proclaim my own praise and not Thine; I would dedicate hymns and incense of triumph unto myself instead of offering them up unto Thee:—*I myself became my own god.*

But whenever it would please Thee to visit me with troubles, whether to try me or to chastize me, then indeed! I knew to remember Thee, not, however, to seek strength and refuge with Thee, the Rock in time of need, but to utter presumptuous complaints against Thine all-wise rule, to accuse heaven, and to exclaim with sinful lips: "My way is hid from the Lord, and my judgment is passed over from my God!"—then I looked with an envious eye upon the happiness of the wicked, whose adornment is pride, and whose garment is iniquity, and who from their heights utter deceit and malice; then I deemed myself forsaken by Thee, who bringest forth the heavenly hosts according to their number, callest them all by their names, and sufferest not one of them to be lost. And thus the very thing which should have been a prop and support for my strength became a snare for me.

And as I thus would be wrecked against my own destiny, so would I fall by the desires and inclinations which Thou hast implanted in my heart: all of them proceeded pure and spotless from Thy hand,—brilliant, clear flames, ever mingling upon the hearth of life to create light and warmth, joy and gladness. Even the desire for evil indwelling within me, is but destined to be conquered by the powerful sword of the holy, heaven-born Seraph within me, and to shine—as the tear of bitter but well understood fate—as a precious pearl in my crown of victory. But did I understand how to acquire this crown? Alas! no—I stumbled and was conquered, I would go after the desires of mine eyes, saying: I shall have peace as long as I shall follow, in my intoxication, the blind impulses of my heart; I would prefer the greedy draughts from the cup of pleasures that end in gall and wormwood and are like unto brilliantly coated decay, I would prefer them to the pleasure that groweth out of close communion with Thee, out of well-preserved human dignity, out of enhanced self-regard and the sweet approbation of my own conscience. Thus I would give myself up unto impure meditations, and sinful desires, so that the flames intended to nourish, sustain and beautify life, turned into poisonous tongues, consuming it with greedy draughts. My folly would seek peace and freedom by casting off the salutary yoke which Thy Law has imposed upon me, and now my soul is like "a troubled sea whose waters cast up mire and dirt."—Aye! even thus far would I often go in my frivolity, *that through and with Thy most-holy name I would wickedly violate the law of reverence to Thee.* Thy name, O Unsearchable One! Thy name, whose honor and glory are proclaimed by the exulting choirs of thousands of voices in heaven, upon the earth, in the air and in the depths of the sea, and which no created being should venture to utter without the deepest awe and the most fervent reverence and adoration,—Thy name I bore in innumerable instances upon my lips as a shallow phrase, without sense and meaning; I would employ it as unto sport, for affirmations that did not proceed from my heart, or also in connection with seriously meant pledges, but which I have never fulfilled; even sinful resolves of anger and passion, of revenge and covetousness, even curses and imprecations so hateful in Thy sight, aye! even the abominations of religious intolerance I sought to seal, to sanctify by the use of Thy holy name.

Also against my *fellow-men* I have greatly sinned, partly by heavy offences, partly at least by not fully performing my duties towards the dear persons united with me by the ties of near or distant relationship,—both towards such as are still among the living, and such that slumber in their graves. The sweet, self-sacrificing love of father and mother, that ever bore me within its heart and upon its arms, and guarded me ever as the apple of its eye—alas! I rewarded it with ingratitude, instead of that reverence which Thy holy Law enjoins upon me. My ingratitude, my indifference, my want of love, pressed tears from the eyes which had watched at my cradle through many nights,—wounded or ever broke the heart which never became weary of holding me entwined with all its fibres, and once set pleasant and brilliant hopes upon the budding child.—Nor would I bestow the proper measure of fidelity, love and care upon the dear, inseparable consort of life and destiny, whom Thou hast placed at my side to share with me in joy and sorrow, and unshaken perseverance, amidst all the changes and storms of my existence. I would not hesitate to wound, by word and deed, the heart so closely entwined with mine,—to violate, by indifference and carelessness, the obligations imposed upon me by the sacred state of wedlock, and I would not seldom be so selfish, as to receive the deeds of the most tender love and undivided attachment with a cold heart, with a gloomy eye, aye! with spiteful indignation.—And no less would I neglect the performance of my sacred duties towards the loved ones of my heart, towards my own children, these precious earthly treasures bestowed upon me by Thy grace. I have been wanting in the *right* care for their education and their future, I have not set them an example to serve them for a shining pattern, I have not afforded them lessons and admonitions apt to make even the rugged path of this earthly life. Oh! I have not done all that was in my power to do to secure their earthly welfare, nor would I, at the same time, pay attention to the promotion of their spiritual and eternal well being. I would be more pleased with their outward adornment than with their inner worth, with the fast vanishing morning hue in their countenances than the everlasting dawn of a pious soul, with their external, glittering garbs than a noble heart, a firm character, and an enlarged mind, I would be more zealous to educate them for the proud pomp of this world than for God and themselves. On the whole, I have neglected to set my house in order, thus to settle all my concerns, that I could depart hence with a tranquil conscience, were it even only in the face of my dearest and nearest.

And when I probe my conduct towards my fellow-men in general, towards the members of the one great family of God on earth, wherewith I may be connected by near or distant ties; when I consider how often haughty words from my lips struck, like deeply wounding arrows, timid and dejected hearts, how often my tongue poured out the deadning poison of slander against the innocent,— how often, when I was in ill humor, aye! even from sheer heartlessness, I drove away from my door the poor and hungry with their tears, or completely pressed their sinking heads to the dust by my humiliating treatment,— how often I threw the firebrand of discord between brother and brother, sister and sister, be it from thoughtlessness, or even from envy and vindictiveness;—when I reflect, lastly, how little I did to advance the salvation and honor of Israel, the prosperity and progress of my Congregation, the beauty and glory of this House of God, but, on the contrary, though one of the race commissioned to glorify the Divine Name, I would profane Thy name and that of Israel by wicked practices, by indifference towards our religious affairs, or through unmeaning, inanimate, hypocritical form and lip worship:—when I consider all these things, then, O God! nothing remains for me but to cast down mine eyes and to hide my face before Thy holy throne, full of shame and repentance.

But no! nothing is hidden before Thee, whom the heavens, and the heaven of heavens cannot contain. But in the dust I will call unto Thee, O my God! and pray: Hide Thou not Thy countenance from me, let me not perish in my sin. I am in trouble—hear me! Draw nigh unto my soul and deliver it from its enemies! God, all-merciful, and gracious, long-suffering and abundant in goodness and truth; keeping mercy unto thousands, forgiving iniquity, transgression and sin, forgive my sins, pardon mine iniquities, grant me atonement. Amen.

PRAYER FOR THE EVENING OF THE DAY OF ATONEMENT. (נעילה)

The day hath turned, the sun has turned and is going down, we approach Thy heavenly gates.

Almighty God! Once more, ere we depart from this sacred place, we would raise our eyes and hearts to Thee, our King and Father, in profound devotion and humility. From the morning we have sought Thee, and Thou hast caused us to find Thee; we have afflicted our souls and bodies, and thou hast accepted this trespass-offering; we have called upon Thee, and Thou hast hearkened unto our fervent supplications; we have longed for peace and consolation, and behold! peace has entered our spirit, and our hearts are filled with consolation through Thy divine grace and mercy. Bent down beneath the heavy burthen of our guiltiness, and conscious of our various iniquities, we entered this Thy holy dwelling place, to spend the day in Thine immediate presence; the morning of this solemn day found us in fear and anxiety before Thee, O all-just Judge! we trembled before Thy judgment. But we prayed unto Thee, O Lord of love and mercy! and confessed our manifold sins and transgressions,—from the depths of our depressed hearts we implored Thee, "O, forgive us, Father, forgive us!"—We turned unto Thee with the solemn promise, never to forsake Thee again; with childlike confidence in Thy compassion we invoked Thy help for the amendment of our ways, and now our souls are become serene, our hearts calm and contented, our minds cheerful and tranquil. We raise ourselves from the dust, for Thy heavenly light of grace and salvation shines upon us, filling us with the beatific hope and conviction, that Thou wilt return unto all them that have returned unto Thee.

Therefore, O God! do we thank Thee for this Day of Atonement and its benefits and blessings. Thanks be unto Thee that Thou hast preserved us to this day, and thus enabled us to perceive, confess and repent our sins. Thanks be unto Thee for the spirit wherewith Thou hast this day filled us, for the sacred vows and resolves which Thou hast caused us to utter before Thee, to begin a new, better and purer life. Oh! do Thou so strengthen and enlighten us, that we may fulfill those pious vows and perform those sacred resolves, that we may never forsake Thee again, or deviate from Thy holy Law, but entirely give ourselves up unto Thy guidance, and follow the paths of virtue and rectitude. Oh! may our hearts ever be filled with fervent love for

Thee, and our souls permeated by profound reverence for Thine exalted name, and unshaken confidence in Thine infinite goodness and mercy, in Thine unfailing wisdom and justice.—As we live through Thy grace and goodness, so make us diffusers of Thy mercy and kindness among our fellow-men, to do good unto all, to feed the hungry, to help the poor and needy, to assist the widows and orphans, to comfort the afflicted, to alleviate the sufferings of the sick, to uplift the oppressed, and thus prove, by our deeds, that we are ever mindful of our sublime destination on earth, that we are truly visible images of Thy being, commanded to be holy as Thou art holy.

And as we now enjoy the delight of Thy salvation, and feel happy at the sound of the voice proclaiming peace: *I, even I, am he who blotteth your transgressions, for mine own sake, and will remember your sins no more*"—"*I have forgiven you*," so let us always find delight in making ourselves worthy of Thy love of Thy mercy, of Thy forgiveness!

Heavenly Father! Do Thou enable us henceforth to live in the spirit of this our ardent prayer,—to behold and enjoy, whenever Thou wilt summon us hence, the peace and salvation which Thou hast reserved for those who fear Thee and love Thee in sincerity and truth,—to leave this sublunary world, as we shall this day depart from this Sanctuary, with our holy profession upon our lips:

שמע ישראל " אלהינו " אחד

"*Hear, O Israel, the Lord our God, the Lord is One in Unity*"—now and for evermore, Amen!

PRAYER FOR THE DEPARTED. (הזכרת נשמות)

Dark and mysterious are the ways of Thy providence, O Lord, for us dust-born mortals, yet, they are just! "When I thought to know all this, it was too painful for me, until I shall go into the Sanctuary of God, then I shall understand their end." But this we do know, that Thy providence rules with paternal hand over all Thy creatures, that even the most bitter afflictions wherewith Thou visitest us are only for our own welfare.

In Thy heavenly household, O God, nothing is done in the wrong place, nothing at an inappropriate time. It was Thy holy will to bereave me of my (*father,—mother,—parents—*) and to call (*him,—her,—them,—*) into a better world· My soul is sad within me, my heart mourns when I think of this irretrievable loss,—when I remember, that my (*father,—mother,—parents—*) who once showed me so much devotion and affection does (*do*) no longer walk with me upon this earth, and that I can no longer reward (*him,—her,—them—*) with my filial love and gratitude. Generations go, generations come according to Thy divine wisdom, in order that this earth may last for ever. I acknowledge Thy supreme goodness and wisdom, yet, my heart bleedeth, mine eyes are bathed in tears, when I remember those dear departed ones that once were my delight on earth, and now rest in their dark graves. But no! only the earthly part of my dear ones rest in the grave, they themselves walk in yonder lucid heights of heaven, where there are no more tears, no grief, no separation,—there they are quickened by the contemplation of the glory of God, enjoy everlasting salvation, at Thy right hand, O All-just Rewarder!

True, mine eye no longer beholds their venerable countenances, my ear no longer hears their soft, instructive and consoling voice, but they, the sainted souls, see and hear me,—their spirits invisibly hover around their loved ones on earth, and every good deed which I perform here below heightens their heavenly beatitude. And thus I may even now bestow my love and gratitude upon my dear departed ones, when I walk in the ways of Religion, when I do no act without asking myself: "Would this be pleasing unto my (*father,—mother,—parents?*"—)Thus I will ever strive to pursue the paths of virtue and morality, to do good unto all men, so that (*thou, my father,—my mother, mayest,—ye, my parents may*) with pleasure look down upon (*thy,—your—*)child from yonder heavenly abode, and perceive with delight my righteous course of life; and whenever my hour shall come, when I also shall rest in the grave from the cares and toils of this life, then (*thou, my dear father, shalt,—thou, my dear mother shalt,—ye, my dear parents, shall*) see (*thy—your*) child again in the realms of glorification, I shall for ever rejoice with (*thee,—you,*) in eternal salvation. Amen.

PRAYER FOR THE FIRST DAY OF THE FEAST OF TABERNACLES.

Lord, our God, and God of our forefathers! Graciously accept the thanks-offerings which with filial hearts we bring unto Thee in the festive commemoration of this day. Thou hast appointed this festival season, that we may rejoice thereon in the blessings which earth hath bestowed upon us in abundance, and, with firm confidence in Thy help, to banish from our bosoms all fainthearted fear and anxiety for further sustenance. Thou willest that man enjoy in gladness Thy gifts for the preservation of his body,—but also ennoble and sanctify his enjoyment by thinking of Thee, the Great Giver of all blessings, by attending to the wants of his imperishable and eternal part, in the remembrance of the high mission of his finite existence upon earth.— All-merciful God! Thy grace is without end, Thy mercy never ceases, every day, every hour is full of Thy loving-kindness; Thou blessest the fruit of our labors and providest all of which we stand in need. Thou bringest up from the dark ground the puny seed and causest it to grow unto thousand blessings. Often the weak heart of man trembles and asks: "Whence shall my help come?" for we are not permitted to receive Thy gifts without toil and struggle, but we must with the sweat of our brow eat the bread that nourishes us. And even herein we acknowledge Thy paternal providence, that we may be guarded against foolish and vain pride, and be fortified in the recognition of our dependence upon Thine almighty protection. But they that trust in Thee shall not be put to shame! "There is no king saved by the multitude of his host, a mighty man is not delivered by the fullness of his strength, Thine eye is upon them that fear Thee and hope in Thy mercy, to deliver their soul from death, and to feed them in famine."

But we remember this day not alone the benefits which Thou hast bestowed upon us, the inhabitants of a flourishing, fertile Eden,—no! with unutterable gratitude we also remember that distant antiquity, when Thy wonderful guidance preserved our fathers in a dreary, barren wilderness. Beneath the protection of Thy tent

Thou didst hide our wandering ancestors against the burning rays of the sun and raging storms. Thou didst refresh them with sprouting waters from rocks and causest streaming rains to descend. Thou didst open the gates of heaven and sent Manna from above for their nourishment,—corn from Thine exalted height. All this Thou didst for Thy people, for Thine elect. Withersoever we turn our eyes, we behold the shining testimonies of Thy mercy, filling us with joy and exultation. Yea, our souls hope in Thee! Thou art our Help, our Shield, our Redeemer! Our hearts rejoice in Thee, we confide in Thy holy name.—And thus, O God! let Thy mercy be ever over us, as we hope in Thee, now and evermore. Amen.

PRAYER FOR THE EIGHTH DAY OF THE FEAST OF TABERNACLES. (שמיני עצרת)

Almighty God! How beautiful is our inheritance in Thy service, what fullness of sublime good hast Thou bestowed upon us, the children of Thy chosen people of Israel! This we acknowledge on this last day of our holy Festivals, while we feel Thy glorious presence within this Sanctuary. For, satisfied through Thy goodness, enlightened through the knowledge of Thine immutable being, we feel ourselves, in this sacred place, free, and elevated beyond all that presses upon us in the tumult and turmoil of the world, and our hearts' deepest longing can but here become gratified. In the midst of songs and praises, our spirits soar up to Thee, to be illumined by the rays of Thy light, to be quickened by Thy glorious majesty, and to be anew encouraged to live according to Thy divine precepts, and labor in Thy holy service, and work for Thy heavenly kingdom, which Thou, O All-good God, didst promise to establish among mankind.

Heavenly Father! Who unitest us with Thee by eternal ties of love, and whom we so often forget in the toils and tumult of the world,—for Thee our hearts are longing, and therefore do we most humbly beseech Thee, to fill us now, and throughout this last festival day, with joy and devotion, that whenever we are assembled before Thee to praise Thy loving kindness,—and during our domestic worship, we may perceive "that the source of life is with Thee, and in Thy light we behold light."

Almighty God! Grant, that this pure festival joy may diffuse its blessings also upon our future life! As once in times of old, our fathers were on this day for the last time assembled in Thy Sanctuary, to offer upon hine altar the gifts of Ttheir hands;—dedicated unto Thee, the earnings of their labors, to be enjoyed not only in the happy circles of their families, but also to be partaken of by the poor and the homeless, the widow and the orphan;—felt themselves moved with exulting enthusiasm at the contemplation of Thine infinite goodness;—as they extended to each other the hand of friendship and brotherly love, and the bond which united them as members of the same covenant, was more firmly tied around them; as they then, filled with delight at all they had seen and heard, returned to their homes, joyful and glad, and determined to walk before Thee in silent memory of those sacred hours, to preserve and manifest all those holy impressions in a life dedicated to Thee alone! so, O God! let the festival joy which this day fills us, henceforth be the aim of all our hopes and wishes; strengthen us in all our labors and exertions;—sanctify all our pleasures and enjoyments, and inspire us to Thy holy service, that we may ever be united with Thee in love and piety; that every knowledge which this day kindles within us, every holy resolve which we make on this Concluding Feast, may henceforth guide us in all our actions, and never cease to teach us that "light is sown for the righteous, and gladness, for the upright in heart."

And when this Festival shall be concluded, and with it all the holy solemn days which we have spent in Thine immediate presence, may we then preserve, and carry with us into life, all the pure and holy feelings, which during those days of joy and devotion, pervaded and sanctified our hearts and souls. May we then return to our homes, glad and joyful, and receive all Thy blessings with gratitude and contentment;—and may all who worship Thee in unity and concord, be united with each other also in their life and worldly intercourse, by the spirit of harmony, love and friendship.

Oh! do Thou fill our hearts with such holy emotions, as will ever induce us to extend the hand of brotherhood all our fellowmen,—wherever and whenever a distressed brother longeth for relief,—an afflicted soul stands in need of comfort and consolation, or the destitute pray for help! then and there make us to diffuse joy and peace, as Thou dost daily grant them unto us.

And with such pious feelings let us again and again return unto Thee, that our love for Thee, our confidence in Thy holy name may be continually renewed and strengthened,—our willingness to serve Thee be enlivened and fortified, and we ourselves united with Thee, both here on earth and in life eternal. Amen.

PRAYER FOR THE DAY OF REJOICING OF THE LAW. (שמחת תורה)

We celebrate this day a sublime Festival of joy, the sacred Feast of Faith and the Divine Law. With delight and love do we listen to the concluding words wherewith the holy Torah addresses itself unto us,—with delight and love do we greet it again upon opening anew its portals. It is the Torah that bestowes upon us richness of heavenly joys, that renders us truly happy. It is the tree of life whose fruits nourishes the eternal spirit and rejoices the pious soul; it is the banner around which all the pious gather, and beneath which all true believers join hands unto a holy covenant;—it is the standard upon which they swear to perform all that is good and holy unto the honor of God and the glorification of their belief; it is the cup from which we drink quiet repose and heavenly tranquillity for the afflicted soul, cheerful hope and sweet faith for the drooping spirit, heavenly comfort and healing balm for the lacerated heart; it is the sun that illumines the dark valley of earth,—it is the light that cheers the gloomy hut of misery and calamity and makes it shine with pure joy in God.

Thanks be unto Thee, O God! and praise and glory, for that Thou hast intrusted unto us such a jewel. We adore and worship Thee, that Thou hast thus enriched and enhanced human life through Thy word, through Thy Law. Without it our life would be a barren, fearful dream, a bark without a guide upon a stormy ocean.

Oh! I feel shocked when I remember what I would be without it, and sacred exultation moves my soul when

I remember what treasure I possess in it. Grant, O Allmighty One! that Thy divine word may ever be alive within me, that it may ennoble and fortify my heart, that it may strengthen me in my faith, in love and faithfulness towards Thee, in sufferings and hardships, in all the trials and visitations that may come from Thee.—May the blessings of Thy doctrine never depart from my house, from my children and the children of my children;—may the brilliant rays of Thy heavenly peace and joys ever quicken and cheer me. Amen.

PRAYER FOR THE FEAST OF CHANUCCAH.

"I will extol Thee, O Lord! for Thou hast drawn me out of the depths." I will sing praises unto Thee, and proclaim Thy holy name. This is a festival of victory, a day to celebrate the dedication of Thy holy temple. Two great gifts hast thou bestowed on us, RELIGION and LIBERTY. Our ancestors had been cruelly robbed of their liberty by the Syrian king, Antiochus, and then they were to be deprived of their remaining good—Religion. For, with sword in hand, the tyrant would compel to idolatry those who adored the Only and Living God, that race whose boast and glory it was to have been the first worshippers of the One and the *Only* God. His presumptuous hand dared to place on the altar of the Eternal a perishable idol. But there lived at that time, also, men who despised a life of irreligiousness and slavery; men whose hearts glowed with the ardor of faith and freedom, who for their God and for truth would sacrifice their *all*, and who, like their ancestor Moses, cried "who is on the Lord's side, let him come unto me;" whose colors bore the memorable words, מִי כָמֹכָה בָּאֵלִים יְיָ "Who is like unto Thee, O Lord, among the gods?"

Mattathias and his sons, of priestly descent—their names will never be obliterated from the book of immortal life—encouraged the people to battle for light in the midst of darkness. And many noble souls, worthy of the name of Israel, were found to rally round the standard of UNITY; to risk the *body* for the *spirit;* to sacrifice *time* to gain *eternity!* and, indeed, the prize was worthy of the struggle. The ancient Temple Service was restored to its full dignity and solemnity; the Temple of the Lord was cleared from all pagan impurities, the altar was again dedicated to the pure worship of the Only God, the sacred oil again burnt clear and bright; and its light reminded them of the heavenly brightness of truth and unalloyed religion, the light that will never be extinguished.

Almighty Creator! May the observance of lighting the candles during these eight days in commemoration of the wonderful deeds which Thou didst perform for our ancestors on those days, at this time, afford to our hearts the light of peace, and comfort, in the hope that there will always be found noble souls in Israel to promote all that is good, even at the sacrifice of their own advantages; that there will ever be found in the House of Jacob enlightened men; that there will always be found women in Israel like Judith who risked her life for her city; mothers, like that mother—Hannah—who rather saw her seven children slain than they should bow before heathen gods. Omniscient Father, let us never lack great minds to peril their lives for righteousness and freedom, for their fellow-creatures and for their country; let us never lack men of vigor who esteem their sacred duties higher than the alluring enjoyments of transient pleasures; let us never lack men of knowledge and learning who fearlessly propound the truth and instruct mankind. Fortify our spirits and our hearts, that we may remain faithful unto Thee under all circumstances of life, that in all vicissitudes of this stormy voyage we may cling to Thee, the God of Truth: So that we may live to dedicate again the Temple to Thy holy name, in the days when our God shall be One and His name One. Amen.

PRAYER FOR THE FEAST OF PURIM.

We thank Thee, O Keeper and Guardian of Israel, for the help which Thou didst afford unto our race in the days of Mordecai, at this season, when Haman, in his malice and revenge, designed to destroy all the Israelites of the vast Empire of Persia, young and old, men and women. The king's messengers had already traversed the country in all directions with the decree ordering the extermination of all the children of Thy people;— the day had already arrived on which the cruel despot intended to gratify his vengeance by a general massacre;—the enemy had already triumphantly exclaimed: "*I pursue, I overtake, I divide the spoil; my lust shall be satisfied upon them! I draw my sword and destroy them with my hand;*"—but Thine almighty hand frustrated the wicked devices of the persecutor and caused him to fall into the very snare which he had prepared for Thine innocent children—they were saved, and rejoiced.

And through whom didst Thou accomplish this great

and wonderful deliverance? Thou, O God, chosest a feeble woman for Thy messenger, for an instrument of the redemption of Thy people, that all the world might learn, how great Thou art also in little things, how Thy power works also in the weak; how that which seems powerless turns triumphantly mighty in Thy hand, that which is fragile and humble, strong and sublime; that we also may know and take to heart, that, however lowly and feeble a man may be, he is nevertheless commissioned by Thee, to do and accomplish the good unto the benefit and blessing of his fellow-men.

O God! grant me also, that my feeble powers may succeed in doing what is good and useful,—that my life may not pass away profitless and fruitless,—that my name may become worthy to be praised and blessed by those who live with me and by those who shall live after me. Amen.

PRAYERS FOR MAIDENS.

PRAYER FOR A YOUNG MAIDEN.

All-gracious Father! Thou mindest and rememberest all creatures with paternal kindness,—Thou guidest and protectest all created beings with paternal hand.

I am Thy child,—Thou lovest me, Thou hast ever loved me, and shalt always love me. Thou didst lead my infancy in green pastures,—to Thee I am indebted for the joyful days of my youth, to Thee I owe all that I am and have. Thou gavest me kind and tender parents to guide, to counsel and help me, whose love and devotion attend to all my wants, and who adorn my life with sweet and precious joys.

I approach Thee, O God, with an humble heart and offer unto Thee, upon the altar of prayer, my childlike emotions, the gratitude of my soul.

Thou seest my heart, it lies before Thee like an open book,—Thou knowest its every emotion,—every thought of my soul is disclosed before Thine allseeing eye. Oh! may all my feelings, thoughts and deeds be pleasing in Thy sight,—may I avoid everything that is displeasing unto my Heavenly Father.

Oh! do Thou direct my heart unto all that is good, whenever it may threaten to deviate from the path of rectitude. Whenever in my inexperience I shall be unable to discriminate between good and evil, let Thy wisdom, teach me to choose aright, that I may ever practice virtue, obey Thy law in truth and sincerity, and walk before Thee in piety and innocence. Oh! grant that vanity may not deceive my heart;—that the allurements of this world may not captivate my senses;—that I may not sacrifice them the precious hours that should be devoted to the performance of my duties;—that foolish levity may not lead me astray to violate the laws of morality and chastity; that the maiden's dignity, the innocence of my heart, may be unto me my highest charm, my most precious adornment.

Bless me, O God! with understanding and circumspection, with health of body and soul, with a cheerful; contented heart. Grant, that I may never violate the duties of filial love, that by no word or act of mine I may offend or grieve my parents,—that I may ever cause them joy and delight through my conduct. May Thy benediction, O Lord! descend upon them;—guard them against sickness, grief and anxiety;—bless their labors and exertions with success, and preserve them unto a happy old age, that they may enjoy a long life, strong and vigorous in soul and body. Amen.

PRAYER FOR AN ORPHAN

My God and Father! turn unto me in Thy love and mercy, now that I am alone and forsaken. The dear guide (*guides*) of my youth has (*have*) left me; Oh! do Thou not leave or forsake me! For thus it is written: "*Father and mother may forsake me, but Thou, O Lord, wilt take me up.*" Whence else should I find help, whither should I turn for assistance, except unto Thee, O Heavenly Father! who art nigh unto all those that are forsaken? Oh! do Thou assist me with Thy great strength and boundless love, and make even the paths of my life, upon which thus early such great obstacles have been heaped, which I am too young and feeble alone to overcome. Teach and instruct me, that I may know Thy holy will and act according to the precepts of Thy Law. Who preparest nourishment for all creatures, who givest food to the young ravens when they cry to Thee, Oh! grant me also food, raiment, shelter and all the necessaries of life now and throughout my life. Grant me strength and power soon to procure myself all that I need, that I may not rely upon the gifts and help of others But so long as I do want these, keep Thou alive the hearts of my benefactors and reward them all their goodness towards me. O God! be Thou with me, I hope in Thee unto eternity. Amen.

PRAYER FOR A BRIDE ON HER NUPTIAL DAY.

All-good God! Soon shall I come nigh unto Thee, by the side of him whom Thou hast sent unto me to be my consort of life;—the solemn moment is fast approaching which shall for ever unite me with the beloved one of my heart. Oh! how my heart throbs,—how it pulsates between fear and hope! For I know the importance and solemnity of this moment; I know that thenceforward my life will assume another form, that I take upon myself new, sacred duties, which are often so difficult to fulfill, as the life upon which I am about to enter, shall be changing and checkered. Therefore, I pray unto Thee from the depth of my heart: Do Thou assist me! Be Thou my guide, my shield and protector upon all my ways! Grant that I may remain united with my companion of life in unceasing fidelity and undisturbed harmony! Do Thou direct all our destinies unto blessings; guard us against all trials and tribulations; strengthen me to be unto him a good and faithful wife; make the days of our united life to be days of happiness, tranquillity and contentment. Yea, O God! grant that our union may be a rich source of virtue, of pious joy and mutual beatitude.

O God! hearken unto my prayer—crown us with Thy blessing, that even in later days we may with joyful and happy hearts look back upon this solemn day and remember Thee with gratitude; fulfill unto me, O Father, the consolitary promise of Holy Writ: "*God give thee the desires of thy heart, and He fulfill all thy wishes.*" Amen.

PRAYERS FOR MARRIED WOMEN.

A WIFE'S PRAYER FOR MATRIMONIAL HAPPINESS.

Lord! bless and preserve that dear person whom Thou hast chosen to be my husband; let his life be long and blessed, comfortable and holy; and let me also become a great blessing and comfort unto him, a sharer in all his joys, a refreshment in all his sorrows, a meet helper for him in all the accidents and changes of the world; make me amiable for ever in his eyes, and very dear to him.— Unite his heart to me in the dearest union of love and holiness, and mine to him in all sweetness, charity and compliance. Keep me from all ungentleness, all interestedness, and humor; and make me humble and obedient, useful and observant, that we may delight in each other according to Thy blessed word and ordinance, and both of us may rejoice in Thee, having our portion in the love and service of God forever. Amen.

A MOTHER'S PRAYER ON THE WEDDING DAY OF HER DAUGTHER.

Eternal God! In Thine endless grace Thou hast brought on this day of joy unto me,—the day of the nuptial feast of my daughter; but I cannot indulge in my joy without uttering my hopes, wishes and prayers before Thee! How often have I in the anxiety of a mother's heart wished the advent of this day, on which my daughter should enter upon the proper sphere of woman, to work and labor as an independent housewife, as a loving and loved spouse. Thanks be unto Thee, O Heavenly Father! for that thou hast preserved my life to see this desired day. And yet, it is not joy alone that now moves my heart, fears and anxiety also seize upon me this day, and glowing wishes, fervent prayers ascend from the depth of my soul to Thy mercy-seat.

O God! grant that love, this great worker of wonders that makes even rugged paths by her charms, that converts barren deserts into blooming fields, deprives the pains of life of their stings and changes earth into a heaven,—Oh!

grant that all-conquering love may ever dwell in the heart of my daughter and in the heart of her husband, for ever to preserve the sweet bond of fidelity and devotion.

Grant, Almighty One! that the house which they are about to establish for themselves may rest upon the strong pillars and props of Thy grace and mercy, and upon the everlasting, imperishable foundations of virtue and piety,— that it may ever be illumined and surrounded by the cheerful light of gladness and contentment,—that both may be blessed with all and in all that conduces to man's happiness and beatitude. Bless their marriage with good and pious children, to grow up like "blooming olive-trees", adorned with all the charms of body and soul, to be a joy to their father and a delight to their mother. Amen.

A MOTHER'S PRAYER ON THE WEDDING DAY OF HER SON.

Almighty God! Thou hast proclaimed that "man should leave his father and mother and cleave to his wife," that he should live for her and pursue by her side the pilgrim paths of this earthly life. Thanks be unto Thee for this day, this solemn day, on which my son shall enter into the sacred covenant with the wife of his heart, with the dear being whom he has chosen for his consort of life. Thanks be unto Thee, above all, that Thou hast preserved him, that Thou hast ever sorrounded him with the wings of Thy grace and love, and hast saved him from the numberless dangers of this life. Oh! be Thou further with him in all his ways and prosper all his undertakings.—Do Thou, who art the source of all blessings and love, bless the union of love which he shall conclude this day before Thy countenance, that he may find that blessing for which he hopes,—a wife that shall always create joy for him, and never cause him grief or woe, a companion that shall persevere with him in all the changes and chances of life;—grant, O God! that concord and contentment may ever dwell between them, that not the smallest cloud may darken the horizon of their matrimonial happiness.

All-gracious Father! One thing more I ask of Thee, in whose hands are the hearts of man, who directest them as streams of water: grant that, though my child shall leave the house of his parents, filial love may never leave his heart;—grant, that his devotion for his consort of life may not weaken or deaden the feelings for those who gave him life, and educated him,—that he may continue to be our joy and delight and preserve that *love* and *reverence* in his soul, for which Thou hast promised *long life* here on earth, and full divine reward in eternity. Amen.

PRAYER ON THE APPROACH OF ACCOUCHEMENT.

O my God! more and more it approaches, the great hour, on which I shall give birth to another being, according to Thy wise ordination. O God! Thou knowest my weakness,—Thou wilt pardon me, that I look toward that hour with dread and anxiety. For Thou, Omniscient One, alone knowest, what that hour shall be unto me. Therefore, I call unto Thee, from the depths of my soul: Fortify me with strength and courage in the hour of danger,—God of mercy! grant that the life of my child may not be my death! shorten the woes and pains that await me,—let Thy help be nigh unto me in the moment of danger, and do not remember the multitude of my sins. Convert, O God! my pain into delight at the lovely sight of a living, well-formed and healthful babe, whose heart may ever be dedicated unto Thee. Lord! have mercy upon me! Into

Thy hand I confide my life,—keep and preserve me from all evil. Amen.

PRAYER AFTER SAFE DELIVERY.

"Bless the Lord, O my soul, and all that is within me bless His holy name. Bless the Lord, O my soul, and forget not all His benefits: who forgiveth all thine iniquities, who healeth all thy diseases; who redeemeth thy life from destruction; who crowneth thee with loving-kindness and tender mercies."

How dark was everything around me but a few hours ago; anxiety filled my heart, and I was afraid of the results of my fears and pains. But when I called in my woe, the Lord heard me, and saved me from my troubles. The hours of anxiety have passed, and now joy and light surround me. Thou, O God! hast safely led me through the dangers of the hour of delivery, Thou hast done more unto me than I ventured to hope; thou hast fulfilled my prayer, Thou hast given me a dear, healthful, well-formed child. Therefore, I praise Thy mercy, and shall never forget Thy benefits; my heart and mouth shall ever overflow with thanks and praises of Thy supreme power and loving-kindness.

And with filial confidence in Thy mercy I commit all my cares unto Thee, trusting that Thou wilt accomplish the work of grace which Thou hast commenced. Thou wilt renew my strength, that I may be able to fulfill the duties of a good and faithful mother.

My God and Lord! Bestow Thy protection also upon my newborn infant, that it may thrive and grow, and be healthful in body and soul, to be a pleasure unto Thee, a delight unto me and my beloved husband, an honor unto all men. Yea, Eternal One! in *Thee* I place my trust, I wait upon *Thy* help; he who trusteth in *Thee* shall never be put to shame. Amen.

PRAYER FOR A MOTHER ON VISITING THE SYNAGOGUE AFTER CONFINEMENT.

Blessed be the hour in which I do again enter Thy Sanctuary, where I may again open my heart unto my God and Deliverer in the midst of His worshippers. Almighty God! here, where so many hearts are raised in unison to adore and glorify Thy name, accept also my thanks and praises. May my fervent emotions, my cordial prayer of thanks and praise be as acceptable in Thy sight as the sacrifice which pious mothers once offered up unto Thee according to the sacred custom of our religion. Upon the altar of my heart I will sacrifice all vain and sinful desires and wishes, and here in Thy holy Temple, in this precious hour, now that my soul is full of devotion and fervor, I will vow all the days of my life unto Thee, Thou Giver of life and salvation,—I will pledge myself before Thee and before myself, to unite all my powers and capacities to fulfill my duties as mother, as wife and as Israelite, and to devote unto them my heart and soul all the days of my life.

Almighty God! graciously accept my vows and grant me Thy blessing, that I may never falter in their performance,—that I may ever find pleasure and gratification in the fulfillment of my duties, and that I shall ever find more delight in doing good than in the enjoyments and pleasures of this world. Grant me wisdom and strength to educate my children to be good and noble men, honest and useful citizens, pious and zealous Israelites. Bless my husband that he may long live among us, that his labors and exertions for our children may ever be crowned with success, and that we may never be in want.—Bless our children, that they may grow and thrive in soul and body, that they may become the pride and joy of our hearts, and find favor in the eyes of God and men. Amen.

PRAYER FOR A CHILDLESS WIFE.

All-gracious God! All that lives and moves in Thy great kingdom Thou hast thus created, that it may be propagated from generation unto generation,—all quickened by the happy consciousness of having fulfilled their duty. A mother presses with joy her child to her heart, smiling under tears she forgets all her woe and pain and struggles with life, full of strength and courage, that she may enjoy motherly pleasures and extend motherly love.—The wild beast, fondling her young, becomes tame, and bears and protects, guards and nourishes her young, and defends them with her own blood.—And even the plant shakes with self-satisfaction its head in the air, and spreads its seeds far around, that they may spring up thousandfold from the soil. But I—I know not these joys, I know them only by sight, but alas! not by mine own feelings and experience;—Thou, O Almighty Father, hast not found me worthy of paternal joys, Thou hast denied me the happiness of calling a child mine own, that sweet bond uniting the hearts of father and mother in harmony and love, which, with its very breath, extinguishes the flame of discord between them, and causes peace to enter their house, and when old age, cold, blossomless old age arrives, and their hearts threaten to shrink, then their child is a twig in full bloom by whose fresh love and warm life they grow young again.

As Hannah, the childless wife poured out before Thee her heavy woe, her wishes and hopes, in fervent prayer, so do I stand before Thee, my God, in the fullness of my grief and trouble, and pray unto Thee, that Thou mayest hearken unto my petition as Thou didst once fulfil her supplication. Oh! may the tree of my life bear sweet blossoms, may my house be filled with the joy of children, my conjugal life be adorned with the blessing of offspring.

But if Thou, in Thine inscrutable wisdom shouldst have so ordained it, to leave me childless, then, O Heavenly Father, I would most fervently implore Thee to grant me strength and courage, to resign my wishes unto Thine exalted will; that I may in humility and submission adore Thy dispensation, and ever remember, that Thou establishest our salvation not alone by that which Thou vouchsafest unto us, but also by that which Thou refusest. May I then also always remember that, though Thou hast denied me a mother's joys, there are yet manifold pleasures which Thou, in Thine endless goodness hast granted me already and wilt yet grant me anew, every day; may I ever remember that, though a mother's duties are not among mine, my life is yet no useless and lost one, and that many other no less sacred and gladdening duties and tasks are bound up with mine existence: the duties of a loving spouse, of a careful housewife, the duty to be a mother to the needy, the oppressed, to be a mother to the lonely orphans,—that I may devote all my strength unto this sublime task, and therein seek and find my joy and comfort. May this be Thy divine will. Amen.

A MOTHER'S PRAYER AT THE CONFIRMATION OF HER CHILDREN.

All-gracious God! thanks be unto Thee for this day,—a day of thanks unto Thee, a day of feast and joy unto me. Thou hast vouchsafed unto me to educate and guide my child with a mother's love and tenderness; to provide him (*her*) with all that he (*she*) stood in need of, and to prepare him (*her*) for the solemn act of this day, on which he (*she*) is received into the Congregation of the believers, to be a member of Thy people, and Thy covenant, to participate in the performance and fulfillment of Thy holy laws and statutes. Thanks and praises be unto Thee, O Father, for Thy grace and loving-kindness!

Oh! do further vouchsafe Thy grace and mercy unto my child,—may the Religion, this gladdening boon of heaven, to which he (*she*) dedicates himself (*herself*) to-day ever fill his (*her*) whole being, that his (*her*) soul may be illumined by the light of truth, his (*her*) heart be inspired for all that is noble and great, and his (*her*) spirit may be strengthened and encouraged for the struggles against the dangers and temptations of life, against the power of sin, passions and allurements, and proceed victorious from these struggles. May love for Thee permeate and inspire him (*her*) all the days of his (*her*) life, that he (*she*) may cleave to Thee with his (*her*) whole heart, with his (*her*) whole might.

Do Thou take possession of his (*her*) whole inner being, that it may become a pure, consecrated Temple unto Thee. Grant that the tender child may grow up and mature to be a strong instrument of salvation for his *(her)* people and country, to glorify his *(her)* faith, and promote all that is good and useful on earth.

Hearken, O God, unto the fervent prayer of a mother's heart. Strengthen his *(her)* body, make his *(her)* strength grow and his *(her)* understanding mature,—make all in and on him *(her)* develop and advance, only preserve the purity of his *(her)* morals, the innocence of his *(her)* soul, the peace of his *(her)* heart, as they now fill his *(her)* youthful being; may he *(she)* remain unto Thee, all the days of his *(her)* life, *a lamb that Thou will never cause to want, that Thou wilt lead upon green pastures, besides fresh, quickening waters.*

And unto me, O God! grant further, and for a long time yet, the happiness to watch over my child, and to delight in him *(her)* with the beatitude and gratification of a mother's love Amen

A MOTHER'S PRAYER WHOSE CHILD IS IN A FOREIGN LAND.

All-gracious Father! far from his (*her*) parental home, far from his (*her*) mother's care and solicitude, my child liveth in a foreign land,—and I who would find delight in watching over his (*her*) health, in guarding his (*her*) every step, in lavishing upon him (*her*) never-dying love and faithfulness, I am separated from him (*her*);—mine eye, my hand, my voice can not reach him (*her*), I can but pray unto Thee, my God, for his (*her*) welfare and salvation. Oh! hearken unto the fervent supplication of my heart, take my child into Thine almighty protection, lead him (*her*) safely with the hand of Thy mercy over every rock and thorn on his (*her*) way; endow him (*her*) with such charms and loveliness, with such prudent and modest deportment as will win for him (*her*) the hearts of men, as will procure him (*her*) the friendship and benevolence of his (*her*) neighbors, and thus turn the foreign land into a home for him (*her*).

Preserve the health and vigor of his (*her*) body and soul, guard him (*her*) against all evil and calamity, against all danger and temptation; keep far from him (*her*) the powerful charm of sin, and help him (*her*) conquer all allurements that may present themselves from without, and to subdue all passions within; that his (*her*) soul may ever remain pure and clear, and cleave, in childlike innocence and piety, to all that is noble and divine, and his (*her*) eye and countenance may ever be a brilliant mirror of his (*her*) spotless heart. O Heavenly Father! grant him (*her*) strength and circumspection, energy and perseverance, to attend to, and fulfill all his (*her*) duties and obligations, that they may be unto him (*her*) for blessing and salvation and make his (*her*) life happy and contented. Help him (*her*) to conquer all troubles and obstacles and vouchsafe unto him (*her*) all that may conduce to his (*her*) present and future welfare.

Hearken, O Father of all, unto my fervent prayer, and bring him (*her*) back unto me, in the right time, full of joy and vigor of life, to be the pride and delight of my heart, a blessing unto all men, and pleasing in Thy sight, my God and Lord. Amen.

A WIFE'S PRAYER WHOSE HUSBAND IS ON A JOURNEY.

My God and Father! God of life, gracious Protector in all dangers! With devout heart I invoke Thine almighty protection upon my beloved husband. His avocations and duties have removed him from me,—the sacred duty of maintaining and supporting his family have called him away from his home. O Lord! do Thou protect him in all his ways! Do Thou preserve his health and life,—strengthen and inspire him, that he may not succumb to the labors and troubles of his avocation. Remove far from him all trials and dangers wherewith journeys are usually beset. Guard him against all mischances, that cunning and malice, falsehood and deceit may devise for him. O grant! that he may find favor in the eyes of all men, and vouchsafe Thy blessing unto all that he may undertake, that his sojourn in a foreign land may be unto our benefit and happiness. Oh! bring him back unto me, unto his home, full of health and cheerfulness, and I will at all times thank Thee, and praise Thy holy name for evermore. Amen.

A WIDOW'S PRAYER.

From the depth of my heart I call unto Thee, O God and Father! let me find strength and consolation in **prayer!**

It pleased Thee, in Thine inscrutable wisdom, to bereave me of my husband, and my children of their father; where, then, O God! can I find consolation, if not with Thee, who directest the cause of all widows and orphans.—I am alone and forsaken, whither shall I flee? To Thee alone, who art the Support of the falling, the Refuge of the forsaken, and the Redeemer of all the oppressed. Oh! with a broken and lacerated heart I stand before Thee, for dark are the prospects of the future; but my hope in Thee is my consolation. Thou wilt illumine the darkness, heal my broken heart and uplift again my depressed spirit. Have mercy upon me *(and upon my fatherless children.)* Let me not fall into the hands of men, to stand in the need of their gifts and presents, but do Thou feed and sustain me, for Thy mercy is exceedingly great. Be Thou with me and assist my feeble strength in the education of my children, that I may safely lead them through the rugged and perilous paths of life into the way of eternal beatitude and salvation. Be Thou their constant Defender, for man has no better Friend, no mightier, wiser and more loving Father, than my God. Be Thou our Support and Helper in time of need. Our eyes are turned unto Thee,—do not forsake us—help us for the sake of Thy holy name. Amen.

MISCELLANEOUS PRAYERS.

A CHILD'S PRAYER FOR HIS PARENTS.

Heavenly Father! Thou art the fountain head of the highest, purest and holiest love, and lookest graciously down upon all pious love. But what feeling of love on earth is purer and holier than that of children for their parents? Thou alone hast consecrated it, hast placed it into our hearts, and commanded us to honor and revere our father and mother, *that our days may be long upon earth.* And for them, the earthly representatives of Thine endless heavenly love, my fervent prayer now ascends unto Thee from the depth of my heart

O God! preserve my dear parents, preserve them unto me, these guardian-angels of mine existence, those founders of my happiness, the greatest benefactors of my life to whom, I owe so much, to whom I am indebted for so much. They have nursed me and attended to me, they have guided and taught me, they have watched and cared for me, they have labored and struggled for me, with their hearts' blood, and raised me up and instructed me to know Thee, my God, and direct my heart to Thee in love and confidence. Led by their loving hands I passed through the bright time of infancy as through a beautiful fragrant garden, full of sweet blossoms and flowers,—every thorn and stone was removed from my paths by their love and solicitude. In all accidents of my life I found at all times the best consolation, the most tender sympathy with them. But I seek in vain to find words for the utterance of the ardent and profound emotions that move my heart. But Thou, O God, lookest into the inmost heart of man,—the most secret feeling speaks unto Thee, Thou Searcher of the inner parts, and that language will reach unto Thee, tho' my mouth may find no words to carry them up to Thee. Oh! mayest Thou grant Thy gracious fulfillment and realization unto my wishes—mayest Thou bless my beloved parents with Thy best, most beautiful and richest gifts, with a long and peaceful life, and cheer them with all the joys and delights of earthly life; mayest Thou make their old age one full of gladdness, free from care and pain;—mayest Thou realize all the quickening hopes that fill their loving hearts, through us, their children. Oh! may this be Thy holy will Heavenly Father. Amen.

PRAYER FOR PATIENCE AND STRENGTH IN ADVERSITY.

All-merciful God! Mine eye seeketh Thee, my soul panteth after Thee, to lay before Thee its heavy woe; the lamentations of my lips ascend to Thy throne. Troubles and sorrows have befallen me and my heart is full of bitter grief. The burthen of misfortune weighs heavily upon me, and however much I may struggle against it, I cannot conquer it. Alas! only in the hour of adversity we perceive human weakness and helplessness and learn, that Thou alone art our support and strength, and what boundless blessing, what infinite benefit Thou hast bestowed upon us by Thy divine law. It is a strong, faithful guide unto us through this earthly pilgrimage, a mild, unweary and inexhaustible comforter in the time of mishaps and tribulations. It teaches us that all dispensations are ordained by Thee, that Thou sendest woe, trials and adversity unto our benefit and salvation.

Therefore do I take refuge with Thee, in the hour of my need, and cleave unto Thee, my God and Father, in faith and confidence. Before Thee I unburden my heart, and offer my tears,—not tears of anger and rebellion, but tears of an aggrieved, mourning daughter,—tears that alleviate the heart, wash away all bitter feelings, and open the soul unto hope and confidence.

O God! Vouchsafe unto me Thy help and assistance,— put an end unto my sufferings and troubles, for Thou art a Father of grace and mercy unto all Thy children: and though we may have deserved, by our own guilt, Thine anger, and Thy displeasure by our deeds, Thy compassion is nevertheless great, and Thy loving-kindness without end. *"Thine anger endureth but a moment, Thy grace lasteth a life-time.*—Grant me only that I may never grow weary or weak in my pious resolves, that I may never thus give myself up unto my pain and sorrow as to become disheartened, and to neglect my duties; that I may never be led away to impatience and irritation, and thus treat those around me with harshness and violence, and that I may never prove regardless of and ungrateful for the least benefit that Thy grace may bestow upon me. Mayest Thou, O God! soon find me worthy of Thy mercy, and of happiness, to send unto me deliverance and salvation, that mine eye may shed tears of joy and thanksgivings. Amen.

THANKSGIVING FOR DELIVERANCE.

Lord of Universe! Permit my humble voice to ascend even unto Thee. Let me approach Thy gracious presence, and pour forth my soul before Thy mercy-seat. O my God! Thou hast been bountiful unto Thy servant, Thou hast blessed me beyond my deserts. Thou hast led me by Thine almighty hand, through all the various dangers, that attend this transitory life, and hast brought me, by Thy signal mercies, to a happy issue of all my troubles. May this Thy goodness teach me more and more to love Thy holy will and adore Thine exaltet name. And grant, O God! that some good end of usefulness my bless my remaining days, so that all my future actions may be pleasing in Thy sight, and that hereafter I may be accounted worthy of Thine everlasting love. Amen.

PRAYER DURING A VOYAGE.

Eternal God! Almighty Creator of the Universe! With profound admiration and devotion my eye beholds the immensity that opens before me. Beneath these billowing waters, in yonder awful deep, a world of beings moves, an unfathomable number of wonders rests; and all these beings, and all these wonders call Thee, O God! their Father and Lord; they praise Thy name, they rehearse Thy glory and majesty,—they exalt Thy greatness to yonder heaven that is expanded over these waters with its myriads of stars and worlds, whose brilliant, luminous forms are reflected thousandfold in the smooth surface of the ocean.

My God! how little do I feel myself, how insignificant, in this immense creation. Full of fear and humility I ask myself: "What am I in this boundless universe, among this endless number of worlds and creatures? *"What is man that Thou art mindful of him, and the son of man, that Thou lookest down upon him?"* And yet, Thou hast exalted him above all other beings, *"Thou hast crowned him with glory and honor, hast given him dominion over the works of Thy hand, Thou hast put all things under his feet."* Yea, Thou hast made him lord of the whole creation, he commandeth even the ocean that containeth mighty monsters, and maketh of its floods a path to carry *him* and his substance.

Yet, all this power of man rests in Thy grace, O God, and in Thine infinite love. Thy hand carries and supports him, whether he passes over valley and mountains, or over waves of the sea; Thy light illumines him, Thy power strengthens him, belief in Thee affords him wisdom and courage to conquer dangers and troubles, waves and winds. But, at a nod of Thy head the earth heaves and trembles, and with it the son of man, the heights and the depths rise, and *he* and his power are gone.

Oh! may Thy mercy never forsake me during this perilous voyage. As Thou didst safely carry the ark of Noah through the mighty waters of the flood, so mayest Thou guide this vessel, that carries me and my companions; surround it with Thine almighty protection, that it may be borne upon the wings of soft and favorable breezes and lead us safe and unharmed to the haven whither we are bound. Amen.

DURING A STORM AT SEA.

May our prayer be acceptable in Thy presence, O Lord, our God and God of our forefathers! and for the sake of Thine attribute of mercy, cause the waters to cease from their raging, and still the waves of Thy great deep. Conduct us speedily to our destined port, for the issues of life and death are in Thy hands. Hearken unto our supplication, even at this present hour when we are praying unto Thee. Calm the storm, and conduct us with kind and gentle breezes. Guard us from the tumultuous billows, and from all the perils of the sea; guard us from the lightning and the tempest, and the confusion of darkness; guard us from dangers by water and fire, and from every obstruction, injury or fear.

From the treasury of the elements, O God, send forth a favorable wind. May all who have charge of the vessel be faithful and vigilant, active and skillful in directing or obeying, that so we may speedily and safely be brought to our destined port. Thou who madest the sea canst still the waves thereof; Thou who didst create the winds, canst allay their rage. O Lord! guard our souls which depend upon Thee, and deliver us from evil. As we put our trust in Thee, let us never be confounded. And as for us all, we will bless Thy name, O God! from henceforth and for evermore. Amen.

PRAYER AT THE END OF A VOYAGE.

Praise and thanks be unto Thee, my God and Father. Again I stand upon dry land, again the kindly earth with all its smiling beauties is spread out beneath my feet. From the depth of my soul I thank Thee, O All-good God! that Thou hast graciously protected me on the dangerous voyage, during which but a feeble, trembling plank separated me from the abyss in whose awful dephts death and perdition are ever lurking! Thou, O God! art the Lord of the worlds, Thy spirit hovers over the waters, Thy grace was my portion. Thou hast safely carried me through rocks and tempests, through waves and raving billows.

Thou didst bind the wings of the storm before whose unbridled rage the dephts of the Sea tremble, and man with all his skill and wisdom stands powerless. Oh! mayest Thou further be with me and guide me safely through all the rocks and billows of life. Mayest Thou guard and protect me against all mishaps. Mayest Thou deliver me from all assaults of malice and persecution, whenever they should rage around me, as also from the destructive storms of passion whenever they should rave and rage within me.

Great, O God! are the dangers and temptations of life; *within* and *around* us allurements to sin and transgression are continually lurking and creeping: but with Thy help we can conquer all temptation, withstand all allurements—Thine is the power, and the strength, unto Thee belong glory, and praise, and majesty, from eternity even unto eternity. Amen.

PRAYERS FOR THE SICK.

PRAYER FOR A SICK HUSBAND.

From the depth of my heart I call upon Thee, O my Lord. Awful is the darkness that surrounds me on account of the sickness of my beloved husband. With a contrite, anxious and lacerated heart I implore Thee, that Thou mayest preserve unto me, yet for many, many years, the precious treasure which Thou, in Thy grace, didst vouchsafe unto me.

Refreshed by no slumber or rest, the nights pass away before me; bitter woe is my severe companion, for the happiness of my family lies prostrate, the crown of my house is sourrounded by dark clouds. O Lord! hearken unto my prayer,—remove this heavy weight from my heart! Do not deprive me of the dearest and highest of all treasures, do not tear the heart from the heart!

But the hope written within my heart, by the belief of my fathers, speaks unto me with consoling words: "Confide,—and endure, whatever the Lord may have ordained for thee!" Yes, I wait upon Thy paternal grace, I trust in Thy mercy, as the sacred bard teaches me: "He that trusteth in the Lord, mercy shall compass him about." Return, O God! unto my beloved husband, his former strength and vigor, return him unto his sacred duties, and let him work, yet for many years, for the welfare of our family! Oh! may this be Thy holy will. Amen.

PRAYER FOR SICK PARENTS.

More in tears than in words is my prayer poured forth this day, before Thee, All-merciful Father! in tears burning and abundant, produced by woe and anxiety! For, what is more saddening for the heart of a child than to know that a dear parent is prostrated upon the couch of sufferings and sickness? And however much I trust and hope in Thy mercy, yet with trembling and alarm I bow before Thee, to implore of Thee the life, the health of my beloved (*father—mother.*) Thou hast proclaimed the word: "*Ye shall seek my face!*" I seek Thy face with a longing heart. Oh, do not hide it from me. Hearken unto my fervent prayer,—let not my tears flow in vain before Thee, have mercy upon my dear (*father—mother,*) quicken (*him—her*) with the soft dew of Thy grace, mercifully pour Thy healing balm upon (*his—her*) wounds, and let the rays of Thy goodness and compassion descend upon (*him—her*) that (*he—she*) may be uplifted by their warmth and restored to strength and vigor. Forgive (*him—her,*) O All-good Father! whenever and wherever (*he—she*) may have erred, and remember all the good and charitable deeds which (*he—she*) may have performed,—Oh! let these deeds now intercede for (*him—her*) before Thy throne of justice and mercy.

May my fervent prayer come before Thee, that the hour of deliverance and salvation may soon arrive, and our tears of woe be turned into tears of joy and gratitude. Amen.

PRAYER FOR A SICK CHILD.

O All-merciful Father! from the depth of my aggrieved heart I implore Thee: spare my child, do not take away this treasure that Thou gavest unto me from Thine boundless grace and goodness. I know, this treasure is *Thine* as all other boons which I call mine; thou disposest of them according to Thy holy will. Oh! may it be Thy holy will to preserve for me this precious jewel! Once Thou spokest unto Thy suffering Congregation: *"Call unto me in need, and I shall hear thee!"* And through the inspired Isaiah Thou gavest the consoling assurance unto Thy people Israel: *"I will pour my spirit upon thy children, and my blessing upon thine offspring!"* Oh! extend this paternal promise also upon my child, grant him (her) health and long life.

And unto me grant strength in all the cares and trials of life, fortify my courage in the fulfillment of my duties and in the endurance of all the heavy burdens that Thy paternal hands may impose upon me. In Thee, O God! I trust, for Thou art nigh unto all who call upon Thee. Amen.

PRAYER IN HEAVY SICKNESS.

O Lord! answer and compassionate me, for I am full of distress, and humbled in mine afflictions. I am bowed down with weakness as a child, and without Thine aid, how shall I bear my troubles? Oh, that my deeds had been worthy of Thine approbation, then had my soul been satisfied and my heart rejoiced. Yet, do Thou, O God! regard my contrition, hear my prayer, and lend Thy mercy even as a staff for my support. O Lord! pains and evils are inherited with the nature of man, yet my soul shall not be shaken by their approach. For, on whom shall I call for help but on Thee? And where shall I rest my hope but in Thy mercies? *"Though my flesh and my heart fail; God i my consolation, my portion for ever; for, lo, they that are far from Thee shall perish, they that go after the favor of others shall be destroyed."* Ah! were my days of sorrow lengthened to the number of mine offences, yet, O Lord! I would still bless Thy name, and Thy dispensations, for Thou art my consolation, the resting place of my soul. Then, wherefore should I complain? I will resign myself to Thy will, for

Thou, O Lord! art the Author of my being, and wilt not destroy the work which Thou hast made. Then shall I profit from my woes, and all times rest in Thy hands; for Thou, O my God! art my Savior and my Living Redeemer. Amen.

PRAYERS FOR THE DEAD.

ON THE ANNIVERSARY OF A PARENT'S DEATH. (*JAHRZEIT.*)

This day recalls to my mind the solemn and sorrowful day on which the soul of my beloved (*father—mother*) departed from its earthly tenement, on which the eye broke that once so lovingly and tenderly rested upon me, on which the hand was palsied in death that once so faithfully guided and supported me—a day of painful recollection, of ever renewed mourning! The ever honored picture of my dear parent appears before my soul, the breath of the sainted spirit is fanning upon me. How could the memory of the glorified being ever vanish from my heart and soul? As long as I shall walk upon this earth, this sacred memory shall be faithfully enshrined within the inmost recesses of my soul, until I also shall conclude my earthly career and meet again the loving and loved being whose loss I deeply mourn.

Father of life! I pray Thee to vouchsafe rest unto the soul of my sainted (*father—mother.*) May (*his—her*) spirit have found peace upon the heights of eternal light,—pure, undimmed peace unto all eternity! May (*his—her*) soul be bound in the eternal bond of life. May it tarry before

Thee in purity and salvation! And for me, (*his—her*) earthly child, who still walks in the shadows of this world, subject to changing fortune, to error and sin, may that sainted soul intercede before Thy throne, that I may be protected upon all my ways and deserve Thy grace. O Lord! Thou givest, Thou takest away, Thy name be praised for ever and ever. Amen.

AT A FATHER'S GRAVE.

All-merciful God! In this silent field, where the earthly remains of my departed father rest, I will dedicate my filial tears and emotions unto his memory. Now, that I have lost him, the dear one, for this earthly life, I fully know what treasure of love I once possessed in him. He, the faithful guide of my youth, my monitor and counsellor, did attend, with wise circumspection to the ennoblement of my spirit and the strengthening of my body; he illumined my mind and filled my heart with love; he submitted joyfully to all *the struggles of life*, in order to procure to his child *the joys of life*. O my dear father—while I remember thee, my tears are streaming forth, and my heart is overflowing with love and grief. But what can my love profit thee now? It can no longer cause thee *earthly joy and earthly happiness*, who art far removed from all *earthly wishes, earthly wants, and earthly cares!*

But doing good, practicing charity, ennobling the heart—these are *heavenly joys* which a child may prepare for his glorified and sainted father. And these joys I will prepare for thee, by performing good actions in thy name and in thy spirit;—these shall be the sacrifices to be offered up by me upon the altar of my filial love,—may God record them in His book of eternal life, unto thy beatitude and salvation in thy heavenly habitation.

O God of heaven and earth! as my sainted father has left behind, *in paternal love*, his blessings, thus do I, in return, *from filial love*, bless his memory before Thee, and pray unto Thee for the salvation of his soul. Oh! mayest Thou also remember him in love and mercy, mayest Thou remember every noble deed, every good action which he performed on this earth, and graciously forgive whatever sin and transgression he may have committed from human weakness. And may all his sufferings, troubles, tribulations and hardships which he had to endure during his earthly sojourn, be his atonement and propitiation before Thee, that he may be a partaker of eternal peace, beatitude and salvation in Thy divine presence. Amen.

AT A MOTHER'S GRAVE.

My dear, beloved mother, who sleepest beneath this sod, for ever laid at rest in the lap of earth—thy child draws nigh to thee with the tear of mourning in her eyes, burning even as on the day when they brought thee hither. Thy spirit sojourns upon the heights of eternal light, but couldst thou ever forget thy child, still walking in the shadows of earth? No! a mother's love is everlasting, eternal, even as her soul is eternal, even as God is eternal who implanted that love in her heart! In pain thou gavest me life, and yet thou didst greet me with a gladsome smile when I lay in thy arms;—thus thou didst ever endure the sufferings of life and accept them with a mother's smile.—What trouble is there, that thou wouldst shun, what care that thou wouldst not endure for me? As thou wouldst watch at my bed of sickness,—as thou wouldst sacrifice all for me,—as thy first and thy last glance at me was full of self sacrificing love,—as thy heart excused even my failings and thy tear shed at my error was at the same time a tear of forgiveness—O sacred spirit of my mother! behold the tears flowing forth from the eye of thy child in the memory of thee,—they are all that I can yet offer unto thee, accept them as a sacrifice of thanks and love!—

Didst not thou teach my lips the first word of prayer and direct the child's emotions up to God? Didst not thou implant pious thoughts in the heart of thy child? Didst not thou guide my first steps in life, and watch over me day and night? Yea, unto thee I am indebted for the germs of all that is good, for the indestructible seeds of piety, religion and virtue! Yea, here I confess it and spread my confession as a lucid shroud upon thy grave.

How couldst thou be separated from me, though removed from this earth? I feel thy presence by the warm stream of feelings flowing through my soul at this moment. Yea, thou dost still bear with me all my grief, rejoicest in my joys, mournest over my aberrations—but thou dwellest in the light of knowledge and truth, and knowest the end, and the evanescece of all that is earthly, and art conscious of the mercy of God and, therefore, at ease on account of all my destinies, and invisibly inspirest me with comfort and courage. Thus then I will again, near this thy sleeping-place, resolve firmly and solemnly, to live in thy spirit, to walk in the path of duty and virtue, piety and religion, worthy of thee, unto thy honor and satisfaction. Whatever dispensation may come upon me, I will endure it in memory of thee, as though thou still didst walk before me, admonish and warn me,—as though thine eye did still see all my actions, until my hour of departure also shall come, and my spirit ascend to yonder heights, there to be received by thee!

Eternal Father in heaven! preserve peace on this consecrated grave which I irrigate with my tears, that the honored remains of my beloved mother may rest therein undisturbed! And unto her glorified soul mayest Thou vouchsafe an eternal abode of bliss, in which the noble, pure spirit may behold Thy countenance in everlasting joy. Amen.

AT A HUSBAND'S GRAVE.

Hither, unto the silent dwelling-place of death, my heart, sad and dreary even as this place, feels attracted. Surrounded by the night of the grave my beloved husband rests here, and my burning tears may flow upon his tomb, my lamentation be poured in undisturbed currents Far from the tumult of life, no stranger's eye, no unsympathetic word desecrates my grief; Thou alone, O my God, art witness to my pain that sitteth in the depth of my soul, so that life with all its beauties appears dark to me, and all its joys seemed to be covered as with a black veil of mourning.

Mayest, Thou, O Father of all, not be angry with me, that I lament thus bitterly, that my soul mourns so deeply over that which Thou has ordained. My God! I do not take upon myself to murmur against Thy dispensatious and to censure Thy ways. Thou art the God of love and wisdom; what mortal could perceive and understand Thee? Who could presume to judge Thy ways and ask Thee: "What doest Thou?" Whatever Thou doest is well done,—therefore do I in the dust adore Thee and in humility pay homage to Thine inscrutable counsel. But can I command my heart that it should not feel my misfortune? Can I say to my grief: "Flee from me!" to my mourning soul: "Be cheerful!?"

And why should my soul not mourn, now that its other half has been separated from it; why should mine eyes not be filled with tears, now that the most brilliant star of my days is extinguished, now that the prop and pillar of my house is broken, the blossom and adornment of my life withered, and the most precious treasure of my heart given up to decay?

But no! only his earthly part, his body, his tenement of dust has been returned unto dust whence it was taken, but his nobler being, his immortal part, his spirit continues to live with all its thoughts and feelings, with all its faithfulness and love. "*The dust returneth unto the earth as it was, and the spirit ascendeth unto God who gave it.*" Thus it is written in Thy holy Book. To this hope and promise I shall ever cleave. The thought that death cannot have altogether destroyed the bond of our hearts shall be my comfort in my mourning, balm to my wounded soul; and as my love follows him into yonder world, thus he will—I am convinced thereof—look down, with his love and his blessing, upon me and my children whom he has left behind in orphaned condition; and as I raise my tear-moistened eye in fervent prayer to Thee, my God, to implore heavenly salvation *upon him*, he will, in return, invoke Thy mercy and grace *upon us*, and thus our souls will meet before Thy throne.

But unto Thee, O All-good Father in heaven! who art a father of the orphans and a judge of the widows in Thy sacred height, unto Thee I confide my life now deprived of its earthly protection, and my children bereaved of their guide and supporter. May Thy love sorround me, Thine almightiness strengthen me, Thy wisdom enlighten me, that I may walk through life strong and courageous; that I may be enabled to fulfill the duties and obligations which are now my lot in double measure, with a manly spirit and a womanly heart, and to preside over my house with understanding and strength, and satisfy all its wants. Amen.

AT THE GRAVE OF A CHILD.

Sweetly slumbering the darling of my heart rests here—my dear, early departed child ; peace unto (*his—her*) soul ! God of grace and mercy ! forgive the depressed heart of a mother trembling in unutterable woe ! Alas ! the blossom that death broke off, was my happiness, and the life which was extinguished at Thy command, filled my heart with cheering hopes. By the side of my darling child, taken away so soon, I hope to enjoy the delight of existence in double measure, to endure more easily all sufferings, and to look towards my end without fear and trembling ; for I hoped that (*his—her*) hand would close my eyes. But Thy thoughts, O Lord, are not our thoughts, Thy ways are not our ways. Thou hadst given me my beloved child, Thou hast taken (*him—her*) away, Thy name be praised ! Yea, even from the depth of my grief I worship Thee with reverence. Whatever Thou doest is well done ; Thou art our loving Father when Thou blessest and when Thou chastizest, when Thou givest and when Thou takest away, when Thou grantest life and when Thou sendest death. Thou woundest and bindest up again, Thou strikest, and Thy hand healeth again. Therefore, I pray unto Thee, Eternal God ! fill Thou my saddened heart with consolation. Strengthen my confidence in Thine alljust ordinations, preserve me in obedience to Thy holy will. Forgive my sins, O Lord ! and deliver me from all evil. Let the spirit of my child enjoy fulness of joy in Thy glorious habitation of peace ; open unto it the source of truth and light, and let it ascend higher and higher in its everlasting salvation. Amen.

AT THE GRAVE OF A BROTHER OR SISTER.

Full of loving recollections I draw nigh unto the grave of my beloved (*brother—sister*) whose memory can never cease. Oh! that thou has departed from me, that thou hast been taken from me, with whom I was united by the most tender bond of blood and love. My spirit wanders back to the days of our childhood which we passed together, in joy and sorrow, with the most fervent devotion and attachment, when, faithfully clinging to each other, we entered upon the paths of life, and strove towards our aim, and endured together, with the most sincere mutual sympathy, all sufferings and trials. Verily! life was of value to us because we enjoyed it together. And though now and then differences of opinion and intentions would separate us, how quickly would we again extend our hands to each other, and forget all! All at once thou wast taken from me—relentless death tore thee from my arms. Thy picture stands before me and fills me with unutterable woe and longing. Alas! thou shalt never return unto me, and I must wait for the time when we shall be re-united. Then thy spirit—as once my hand,—will seize mine, and lead me up, and show me the way unto purer light, unto higher joys.—O Lord! may my (*brother's—sister's*) spirit have attained to eternal peace, that (*his—her*) heart, satisfied by Thy river of love, be filled with the highest clearness and cheered by the highest salvation! Peace be unto this consecrated spot that contains these remains. Amen.

www.ingramcontent.com/pod-product-compliance
Lightning Source LLC
Chambersburg PA
CBHW020150170426
43199CB00010B/971